THE CONFUSION ERA

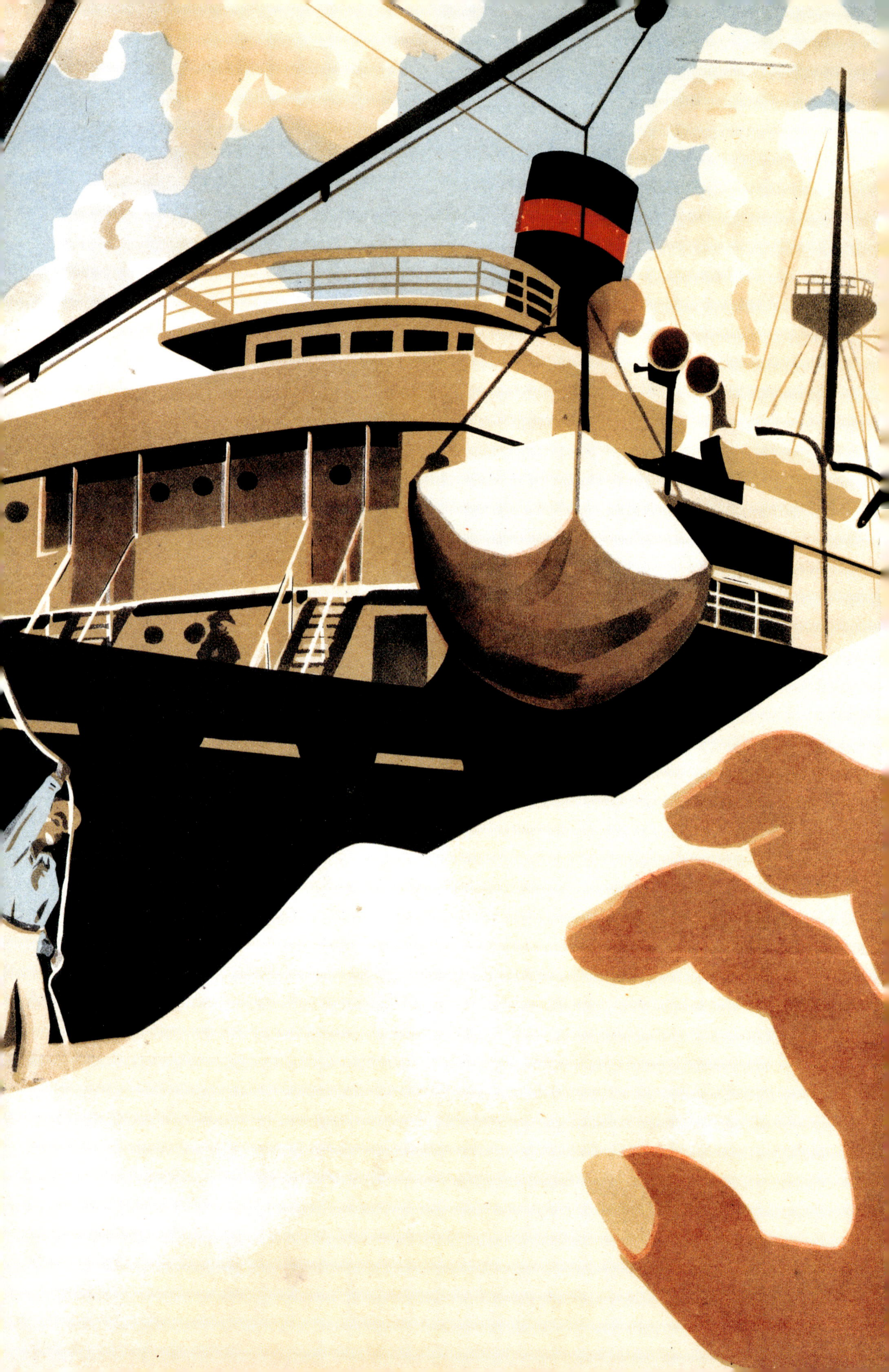

The Confusion Era

ART AND CULTURE OF JAPAN DURING THE ALLIED OCCUPATION, 1945–1952

Edited by **Mark Sandler**

Arthur M. Sackler Gallery, Smithsonian Institution

in association with the **University of Washington Press,** Seattle and London

Published by the Arthur M. Sackler Gallery, Smithsonian Institution, Washington, D.C., in association with the University of Washington Press, Seattle and London.

Printed in Hong Kong

This publication was supported in part by the Donald R. Ellegood International Publications Endowment.

Cover: (top) Horace Bristol, *Off Limits,* 1946 (detail); black and white silver gelatin print; (bottom) Omi Takashi, "Shiseido Cosmetics," 1946 (detail); see page 75.

Frontispiece: Tani Masuzo, "Don't Sell Salt Illegally. The World Is Monitoring Imported Salt," 1950 (detail); see page 83.

Library of Congress Cataloging-in-Publication Data
The confusion era: art and culture of Japan during the Allied Occupation, 1945–1952 / edited by Mark Sandler.
p. cm. — (Asian art & culture)
Includes bibliographical references and index.
ISBN 0-295-97646-2 (pbk.: alk. paper)
1. Arts, Japanese—20th century.
2. Arts and society—Japan—History—20th century.
3. Japan—Civilization—American influences.
4. Japan—History—Allied occupation, 1945–1952.
I. Sandler, Mark Howard, 1945– . II. Series.
NX584.A1C66 1997
700'.952'09044—dc21 97-18946
CIP

The paper used in this publication meets the minimum requirements for the American National Standard for Permanence of Paper for Printed Library Materials, Z39.48–1984

Photo credits

Cover (top) and pp. 10, 13, 14, 16, 19, 90, 95, 98: © Horace Bristol. Reproduced with permission; p. 12: Reproduced from the Collections of the Library of Congress, Washington, D.C. Prints & Photographs Division, LC-USZ6-1587; p. 17: © Freer Gallery of Art, Smithsonian Institution; pp. 26–35: courtesy Tokyo National Research Institute of Cultural Properties; pp. 38, 44, 45: by permission of Nikkatsu Corp., Tokyo / p. 44 courtesy East-West Classics, Piedmont, CA; pp. 41, 42, 46, 49: by permission of Ace Pictures, Inc., Tokyo; pp. 52–69: courtesy Kawakita Memorial Film Institute, Tokyo; pp. 73, 75: by permission of Shiseido Co., Ltd., Tokyo; pp. 74, 77: courtesy Imatake Shichiro; pp. 76, 78–80, 87: courtesy Musashino Art University, Museum and Library; pp. 81–83: courtesy Tobacco and Salt Museum, Tokyo; pp. 84, 85: courtesy Kono Takashi; p. 88: courtesy Arthur M. Sackler Gallery, Smithsonian Institution (AMSG, SI), from *100 Best Japanese Posters* (Tokyo: Toppan Printing Co., Ltd., 1990) with permission of the publisher; p. 86: by permission of Hayakawa Yoshio/courtesy AMSG, SI, from *100 Best Japanese Posters;* p. 92: courtesy Sherman E. Lee; p. 93, 97: U.S. Army Signal Corps photos / courtesy Donald Richie; p. 99: by permission of Nomura Art Museum, Kyoto / courtesy AMSG, SI; p. 101: courtesy AMSG, SI.

Contents

Foreword

MILO CLEVELAND BEACH

The Allied Occupation, immediately following the end of the Second World War, witnessed profound American involvement in virtually every aspect of life in Japan, forever changing the dynamic between the countries. Numerous studies addressing politics, economic and constitutional development, and education reform have been published but little has been written concerning the conditions of the arts during this formative era. As the world marks a half century since the events of the Occupation, it is time to reflect on the creative environment that affected the cultural and social life of the country. *The Confusion Era: Art and Culture of Japan During the Allied Occupation, 1945–1952,* brings together an eminent, lively group of authors for a critical exploration of the achievements and experiments of this crucial time.

Film historian and writer Donald Richie's "The Occupied Arts" probes the ironies, missteps, and politics of the Occupation censors and their new colleagues in the Japanese cultural community. Citing incidents both famous and infamous, the essay deftly touches on painting, theater, and film, including such examples as Kurosawa Akira's *They Who Step on the Tiger's Tail* (Tora no o o fumu otokotachi)—which was prohibited by the Japanese authorities as too democratic, then banned by the American authorities as too feudalistic, and the release of the film had to wait until the end of the Occupation.

Artist Kitawaki Noboru's *Quo Vadis* (1949) depicts a man uncertain of which way to go; a long queue of people stirs memories of lines of soldiers, or captives, while the blue of the sky suggests endless emptiness. This painting mirrors the absorbing issues facing visual artists who not only suffered reversals of fortune during the war but also a fundamental confusion of values in the aftermath. Many venerable artistic approaches fell into disrepute after the war. Some artists actively sought an international style, while others attempted to overcome the harsh realities of daily existence through heroic acts of expression. In a revealing look at nine artists, Emiko Yamanashi surveys the results of the caution and experimentation of the era.

Keiko I. McDonald examines the conflicted and provocative evolution of women's roles in film in her essay "Whatever Happened to Passive Suffering?" while Linda C. Ehrlich discusses two films by Japanese directors looking back on the period. The Americans were attempting to instill new values—for example, by promoting "the individual" as opposed to the traditional Japanese focus on "the group." Democracy was "everywhere," but no one could be sure what it would mean for the Japanese as when, in one film scene, a student nervously responds to the new prescription for coed classrooms with the question: "Is that democracy?"

Emergency food and health announcements had to be printed despite extreme shortages so severe that locating sheets of paper large enough for posters required extraordinary effort. In tandem, production of posters for movie and commercial advertising never ceased either. Some of the paper was of such poor quality that only the ink used in the lithographic process held it together. Ranging in purpose from soliciting donations of clothes to promoting cosmetics and "Peace Cigarettes," a selection of posters forms a portfolio, assembled by James Howard Fraser.

Closely connected with American efforts to foster Japanese cultural patrimony during the months immediately after surrender, Sherman E. Lee provides a telling first-person account of his experiences during those difficult years. His job with the Arts and Monuments Division of the Supreme Commander of the Allied Powers (SCAP) in Tokyo led him to inspection visits of temple sites and art collections in many parts of Japan at a time of intense national scrutiny.

The Allied Occupation of Japan was the bridge between a period of wartime distrust and carnage and today's productive, culturally rich interdependence. *The Confusion Era* is the first in "Asian Art & Culture," a series of books that integrate the perspectives of writers, art and cultural historians, artists, and literary scholars on critical themes in Asian art and culture. ●

Note: Japanese names are given in Japanese order, surname first.

Acknowledgments

The Confusion Era evolved as the result of the energy and commitment of many people. Milo Cleveland Beach, director, and Thomas W. Lentz, deputy director, of the Arthur M. Sackler Gallery and the Freer Gallery of Art, have been steady sources of support and advice. The editors wish to thank J. Thomas Rimer, of the Department of East Asian Languages and Literatures, University of Pittsburgh, for editing and adapting Emiko Yamanashi's essay and for his many ideas concerning the content and authors for this book. James T. Ulak, curator of Japanese art, Arthur M. Sackler Gallery and Freer Gallery of Art, and Yasuhiro Oka, research assistant, translated the exhibition catalogue for the Hakutsuru Museum exhibition held in April 1947 in Kobe and prepared the sidebar accompanying Sherman Lee's essay. Ann Yonemura, associate curator of Japanese art, reviewed texts and consulted with the editors, and Reiko Yoshimura, librarian, provided continuous assistance checking and translating Japanese.

The thoughtful expertise of editors Ann Hofstra Grogg, Susannah Gardiner, and Mary Cleary greatly enhanced the presentation and substance of the text and illustrations while Carol Beehler's vigorous, off-center design skillfully evokes the era. The editors also thank Loi Thai, publications assistant, for his invaluable and careful work; Michelle Smith, indexer; and Susan Bliss, head of public affairs. Karen Sagstetter, editor in chief, provided editorial direction and critical guidance during the development and production of the book. The editors are grateful to colleagues at the University of Washington Press, especially Pat Soden, director; Veronica Seyd, assistant director and production manager; and Don Ellegood, director emeritus, whose enthusiastic commitment brought *The Confusion Era* to fruition. ●

—M.S.

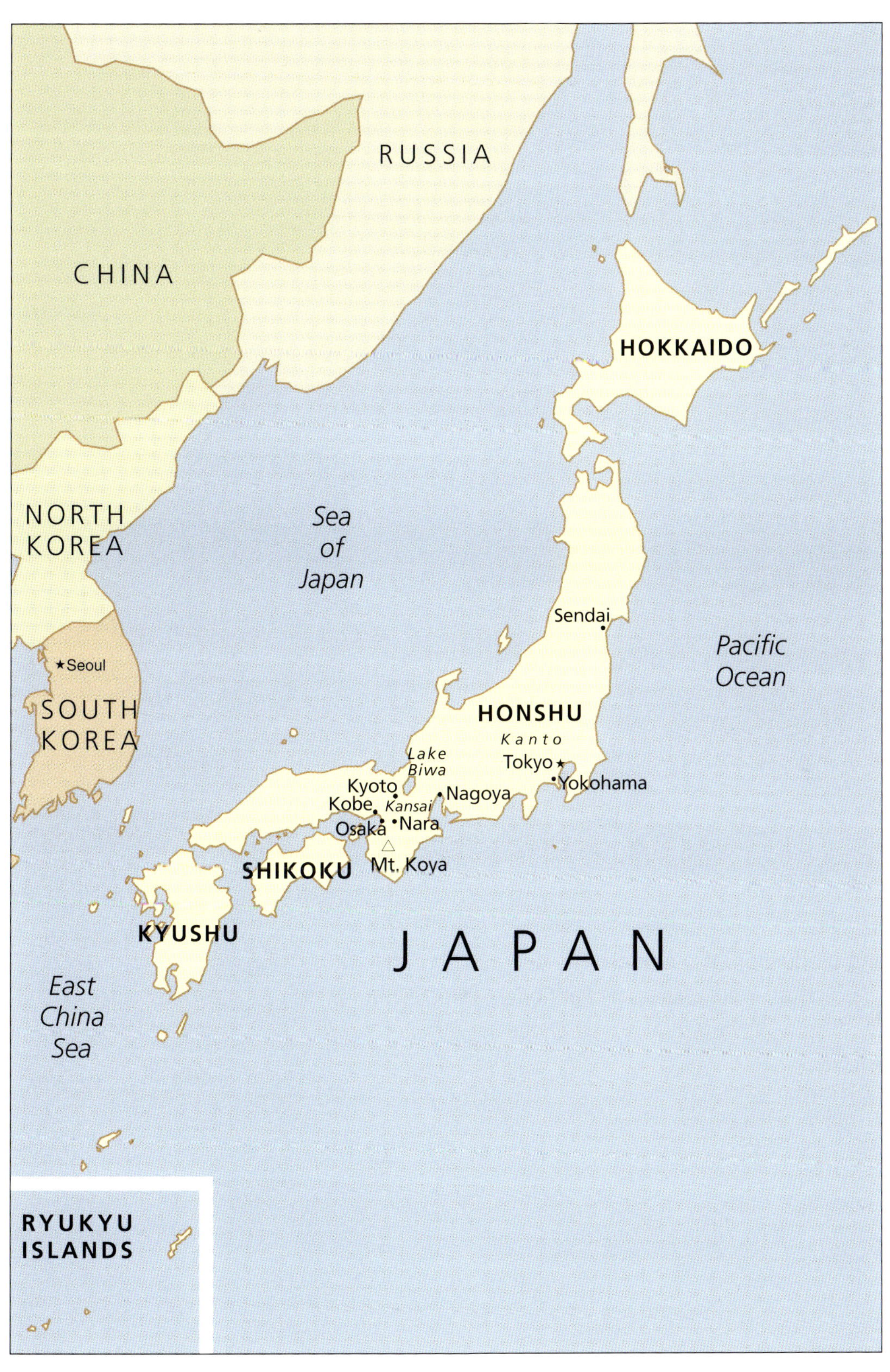
RUSSIA
CHINA
HOKKAIDO
NORTH KOREA
Sea of Japan
Sendai
Pacific Ocean
Seoul
SOUTH KOREA
HONSHU
Kanto
Tokyo
Yokohama
Lake Biwa
Kyoto
Nagoya
Kobe
Kansai
Osaka
Nara
Mt. Koya
SHIKOKU
KYUSHU
JAPAN
East China Sea
RYUKYU ISLANDS

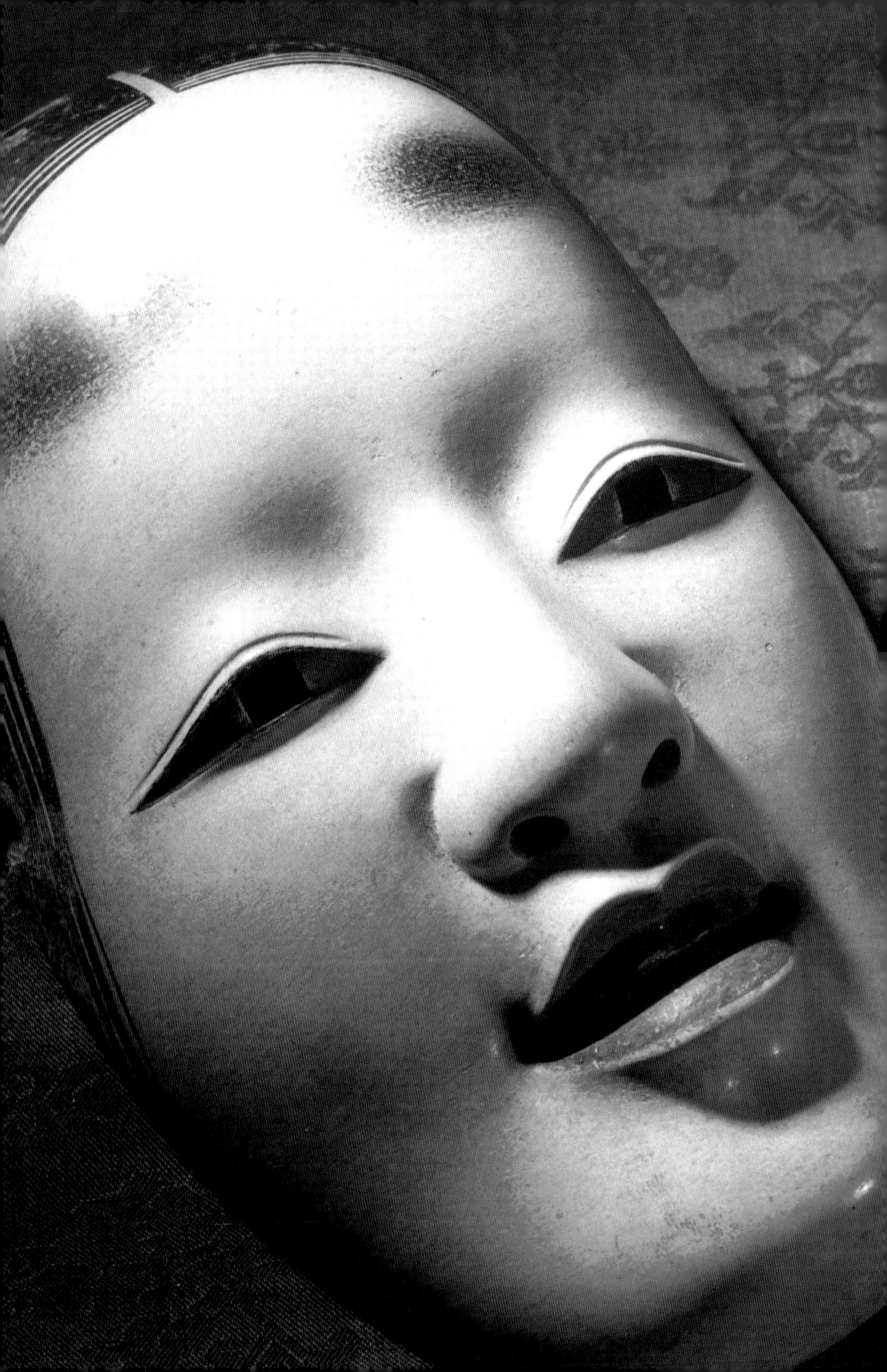

The Occupied Arts

DONALD RICHIE

The Allied Occupation of Japan after World War II, though it lasted only seven years, brought about the kind of sudden social change that is rare in Japanese history. Along with the Taika Reform of 645 and the Meiji Restoration of 1868, the Occupation has rightly been called "one of the three main periods in which Japanese self-consciously adopted institutional reforms from abroad."[1]

The Occupation — the military and political control of Japan by the United States and, to a much lesser degree, its World War II allies — technically began with Japan's surrender on August 15, 1945, and ended with the enforcement of the San Francisco Peace Treaty on April 28, 1952. In reality, elements of the Occupation still exist in the form of U.S. troops on Japanese soil, and the 1945–52 Occupation has left a dappled legacy. Even now, half a century later, the Occupation's aims, methods, and accomplishments still raise questions both in Japan and in the United States.

For those seven years, power in Japan rested with the Supreme Commander of the Allied Powers (SCAP), which has been described as "a supra-constitutional authority using unavoidably dictatorial methods to establish democratic rights in Japan."[2] As an occupation, however, this one was surprisingly benign. It was (originally, at any rate) devoted to the creation of a new society that would be humane, peace-loving, and democratic: in a word, American. This new country was to be placed — forcibly, if necessary — on top of a country perceived in many ways as its opposite.

As it turned out, America's urge to educate and, if necessary, to preach found ready fulfillment in this beaten archipelago. Japan's citizens were willing pupils who had backed the wrong model and were now eager to try out the new.

CENSORSHIP AND THE SUPREME COMMAND

The agenda that properly occupied SCAP, in particular its Civil Information and Education Section (CIE), was entirely political, economic, and social. As such, though the Supreme Commander had much to say about the media, the documents establishing SCAP mentioned little about the arts. None of the planning documents contain anything pertaining to

Horace Bristol, *Noh Mask of Young Woman,* 1946. Black and white silver gelatin print.

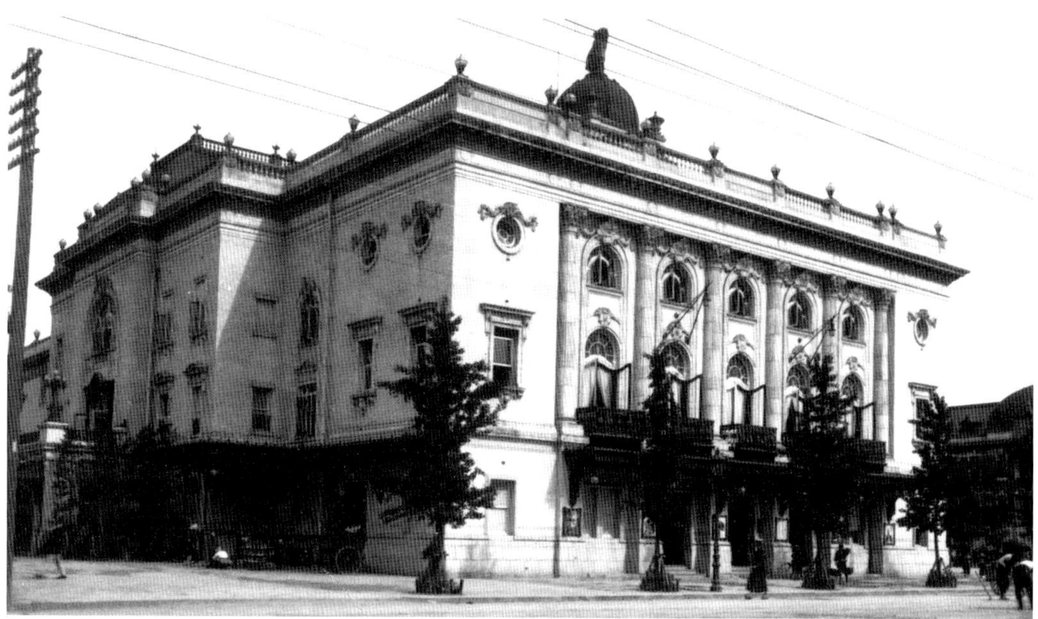

With the Allied Occupation came heavy censorship of Japan's traditional Kabuki theater. Performances were held at Tokyo's Imperial Theater, shown here in a circa 1925 photo.

culture, except for radio and the movies, and neither of these was considered anything other than media.[3]

Even so, the arts were not left unexamined, and some — particularly film — were censored by the CIE. Painting, sculpture, literature, and modern drama, though spared outright censorship, were liable to discipline through "guidance." In theory separate, these two methods of control were both coercive. CIE opinion ("guidance") carried all the weight of its official disapproval ("censorship").

Ironies naturally abounded: SCAP labored to promote democracy in Japan but banned all criticism of its own workings; cartoonists in this newly free society were forbidden to make caricatures of the Supreme Commander; liberated filmmakers were not permitted to film or depict the occupiers, or even to show glimpses of Mount Fuji, which was perceived by these occupiers as an imperial symbol; anything "feudal" was searched out and uprooted, yet the emperor and much of the imperial system were allowed to remain.

Nonetheless, the Occupation was noticeably idealistic, indeed high-minded. With enthusiasm, patience, and occasional tact the occupiers began their great educational adventure. It was an all-American show. Though the A in SCAP stood for Allied, in practice the Allies were shoved elsewhere, and the A came to stand for American. The new imperial government was the USA, with General Douglas MacArthur, just across the moat, as its uncrowned emperor.

THE VISUAL ARTS

SCAP was a new broom that swept clean many a corner, yet its promulgations only rarely mentioned the arts. Many artists had enthusiastically and often visibly supported various Japanese wartime propaganda efforts, in particular the activities of the Greater

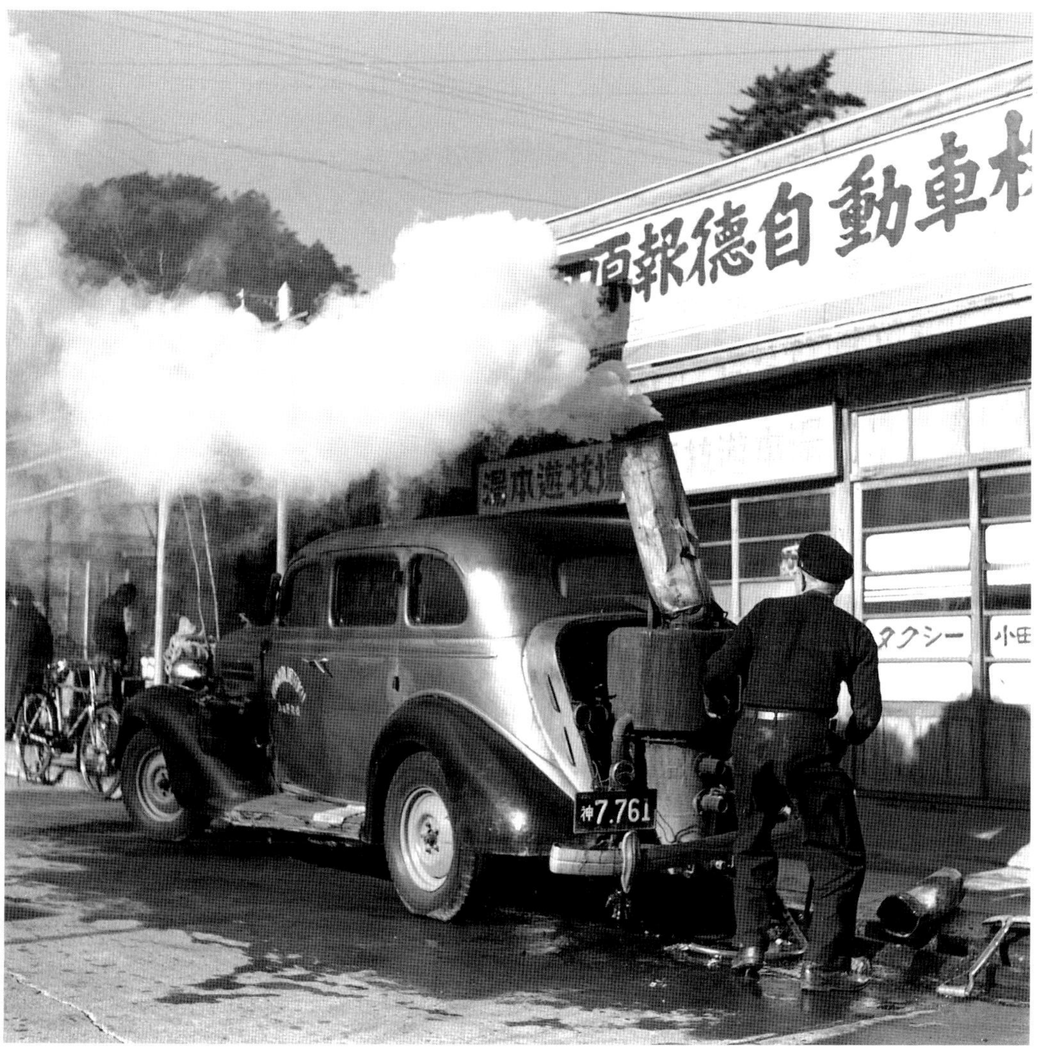

Horace Bristol, *Charcoal Burning Automobile in Tokyo Street*, 1947. Black and white silver gelatin print.

East Asia Co-Prosperity Sphere, which served to designate Japan's imperial designs. While politicians, the military, industrial magnates, and even martial arts experts were eventually purged, no painters or sculptors ever were.[4]

Those painters who had openly supported Japanese militaristic policies were never called to account, and indeed such wartime activities are now usually left out of their official biographies. Yokoyama Taikan, who had even (among much else) delivered a 1938 lecture on the spirit of Japanese art to a visiting group of Hitler Youth, continued to exhibit just as though nothing had happened. Painting, along with most other arts, was marginalized to the point of irresponsibility.

When SCAP did occasionally take notice of artistic endeavor, its efforts were uncoordinated. In the spring of 1947 it ordered that a draft proposal, *Essentials for the Guidance of Study: Arts and Crafts* (Gakushu shido yoryo: Zuga kosaku hen), be outlined by the Ministry of Education. Wartime textbooks for the teaching of art were sternly banned, but new texts were not approved until 1951, by which time the Occupation was practically over. In the meantime, SCAP frowned on paintings of bombers, warships, or imperial shrine archways.

Artists were otherwise left to their own devices. Many went abroad to see what had happened to art during the war. Those at home had to wait for new art to arrive in Japan. Though Mitsukoshi Department Store held a showing of reproductions of modern French paintings in 1948, the first Matisse and Picasso exhibitions did not arrive until 1951. The West had to wait even longer to see any new Japanese art. In 1948, for example, the Museum of Modern Art in New York refused to exhibit Japanese children's art because of its allegedly fascist connotations.[5]

LITERATURE

Benign neglect also permeated the Occupation's attitude toward literature and contemporary drama. The members of the CIE would openly push those American authors they thought best embodied American ideals, but overt censorship was uncommon. What the CIE did censor, it tended to forbid totally — for instance, the wholesale ban on any Japanese translation of Steinbeck's *Grapes of Wrath.*

On the other hand, there was little in new Japanese literature to censor. After years of wartime controls, the sudden release of Japanese military censorship rules resulted in an explosion of ephemera, largely the erotic nonsense called *eroguro* in Japanese (from the English words "erotic" and "grotesque"), which posed no political threat.

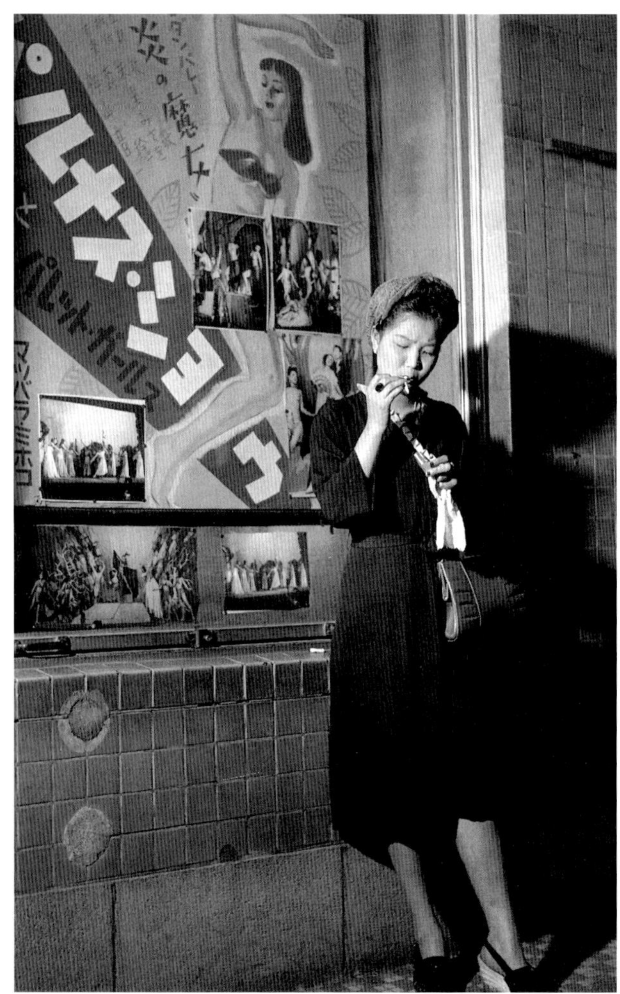

Horace Bristol, *"Angel of the Night" Waiting for Customer in Tokyo Subway,* 1946. Black and white silver gelatin print.

What literary censorship occurred was usually handled by the Japanese themselves, under Allied orders. This arrangement gave the illusion of local responsibility, and it kept SCAP out of trouble in case there were repercussions. It was indeed a very Japanese way of doing things and is perhaps one of the earliest instances of the conquerors learning from the conquered, rather than the other way around.

Also, since the Occupation was primarily a bureaucracy, and since the Japanese offices under its command were eager to demonstrate dedication, SCAP managed to exercise an amount of censorship indirectly, through simple advice from its own Civil Censorship

Detachment (CCD). Among works thus tampered with were Japan's oldest chronicle, the *Kojiki,* several of Natsume Soseki's works, a story by Tanizaki Junichiro, one of Yokomitsu Riichi's novels, and — mysteriously — Tolstoy's *War and Peace.*[6]

The manner in which this censorship was accomplished has occasioned criticism: it was done in secret. SCAP never revealed at the time that its officers' "advice" to book publishers (and to theater and movie producers) was really orders. "We were refused the knowledge that the Japanese materials were even being censored," one American critic later complained, "whereas the prewar Japanese censors had made no effort to disguise the process."[7]

Though some, such as the Japanese literary critic Eto Jun, have maintained that the Occupation attitude toward literature was such that "the Japanese spirit" was lost in the flood of sensational postwar literature, it is difficult to blame this loss on the occupiers. Literature was too low on their list of priorities to ensure such attention.

The Occupation's literary activities were more ad hoc than a planned suppression of "the Japanese spirit." The SCAP officers, according to American scholar Jay Rubin:

> **reflected America's ambivalent attitude toward the atomic bombings by initially making it difficult for Japanese writers to publish some of their more intense expressions of outrage, though many of these appeared in print long before the Occupation was over. They changed a lot of references to "the enemy" in war stories to "the Americans." And, in the most systematically practiced distortion of postwar reflections of contemporary life, they consistently suppressed descriptions of GIs holding hands with Japanese women.**[8]

This last activity commanded a surprising amount of attention. In the early Occupation there were notices posted: "No Fraternization with the Indigenous Personnel." And there was the celebrated "six-inch rule" of a general by the name of Swing. This was a calibrated measure that MPs were instructed to insert between GIs and their dancing partners at the Ginza Mimatsu and the other dance halls that were allowed.

Since the indigenous personnel were also known to swarm at movie houses, theaters, cabarets, and coffee shops, entry to such places was forbidden the soldiers except on those special occasions when a venue was, for the evening, put off-limits to Japanese and filled with Occupation personnel enjoying so-called geisha dancing or carefully laundered Kabuki.

MODERN DRAMA

Though all traditional Japanese drama, particularly the Kabuki, was much censored during this period, modern drama, or the Shingeki, was, like literature, left alone. Modern drama had long had an important cultural role in Japan; one literary critic has said that in the first months after the war, the Shingeki "became the center, not only of the theater world, but of Japanese culture as a whole."[9]

Perhaps noting this, the CIE began to pay attention — at least to the point of arranging translation and performance rights for some sixty American plays and then encouraging performance. This effort satisfied the occupiers' self-interest and fitted in with their aims to democratize the country. In addition, some of the plays (Thornton Wilder's *Our Town,* for example) happened in their own right to be quite good.

Usually when such pressure was applied by the Occupation it was, in true Japanese fashion, applied obliquely. The Japanese Ministry of Education was ordered to do the work while the CIE, who ordered it, remained invisible.

In the case of the selling of Wilder's next play, *The Skin of Our Teeth,* however, the pretense was dropped. A member of the CIE summoned all Shingeki troupe heads, sat them down, made them listen to a reading of a translation of the play, and then "browbeat and ridiculed" the assembled company in an attempt to force the American play down the Japanese throat. (This forceful member of the CIE's Informational Division, Motion Picture and Theatrical Branch, has been identified as one Hal Thompson, a former actor.) Not only was the 1948 production a great failure, but this high-handed treatment of the Shingeki leaders led to much distrust.

Resentment was compounded by the CIE's error of not allowing the Haiyuza Troupe to stage a 1949 play by Suzuki Masao, *The Human Bindery* (Ningen seihon) and insisting instead upon John Van Druten's *Voice of the Turtle.* The Suzuki play's sub-

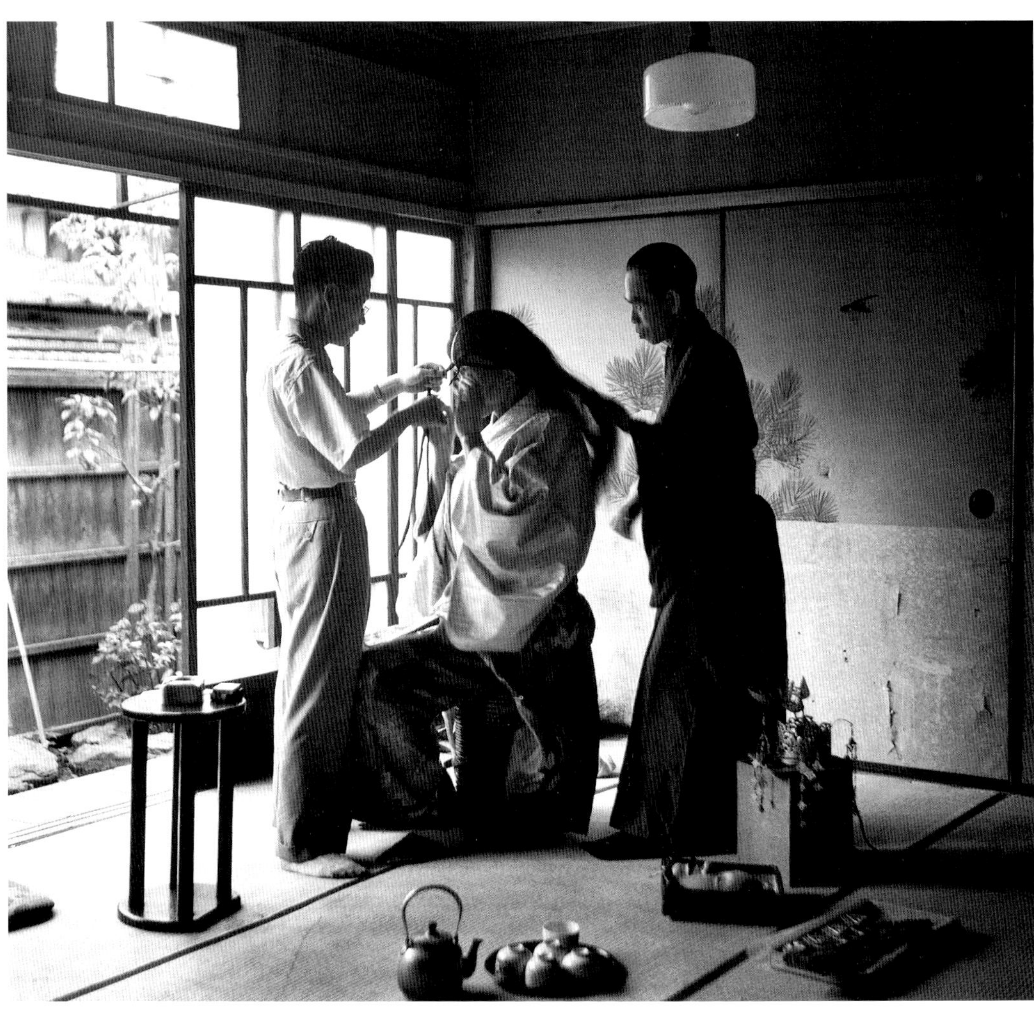

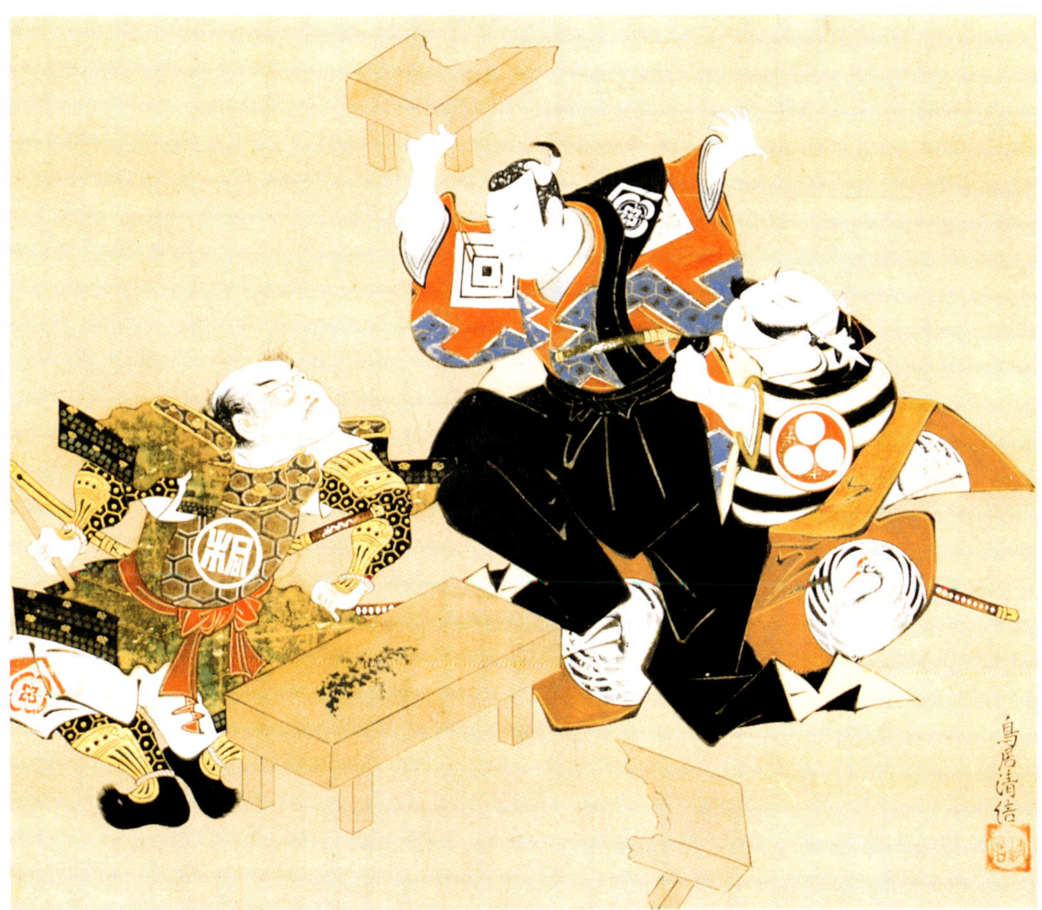

ject matter — a bunch of bookbinders acquire class consciousness and decide to strike — was the reason for the substitution of the Van Druten play, in which nothing of the sort occurs.

Early on, SCAP, with a wary eye on the Soviet Union, had decided to clamp down on the communists, and anyone who went on strike was automatically seen as communist. This fear managed in midstream to turn the direction of the Occupation from suppressing the military and punishing war criminals to having second, more favorable thoughts about the usefulness of standing soldiers and the efficacy of gathering expertise from war criminals. The Shingeki would be closely examined for "leftist" tendencies until the end of the Occupation. The only Japanese playwright actually purged was Kishida Kunio, one of the Shingeki's founders.[10] His "crime" was "collaboration," and he was also — two birds with one stone — perceived as a leftist.

Torii Kiyonobu I, *Scene from a Kabuki Play.* Japan, Edo period (1615–1868). Hanging scroll; ink, color, and gold on paper, 41.0 x 52.6 cm. Freer Gallery of Art, 98.14

Left: Horace Bristol, *Dressing Noh Dancer,* 1947. Black and white silver gelatin print.

THE KABUKI

The Shingeki itself, however, was, like the Noh and the Bunraku, judged by SCAP an innocent if occasionally misled art. On the whole, it was considered salvageable. This assessment was much different from the view of the demonized Kabuki, which was considered, as David Goodman has said, "sinister and a real threat to the re-education of the Japanese people." For that reason, Goodman adds, "the Occupation came down very hard on it."[11]

One of the most dramatic moments in that crackdown on the Kabuki came in September 1945, when Japanese police officers and American MPs walked onto the stage of the Imperial Theater and stopped a performance of *Terakoya*.[12] The Japanese police probably preceded the American MPs, since even this early it was American policy that the Japanese should be seen doing the policing.

Many in the Occupation were appalled at SCAP's ignorant official attitude toward the Kabuki, which made it the scapegoat for all so-called feudal tendencies. Many, such as aide-de-camp Faubion Bowers, were vocal in their outrage. Others, such as his superior, the late Earle Ernst, who was in charge of concerned section of the CCD and is now remembered as the preeminent Kabuki scholar in the West, were both more temperate and more practical.

Ernst worked toward a gradual liberation of the Kabuki from the enormous onus under which it had been placed. He early on "liberated" the part of the repertoire deemed "nonfeudal" and then tried to save such works as *Terakoya*. In so doing he countered both the excesses of the officers above him and the kowtowings of companies like Shochiku, which ran the Kabuki and which during the Occupation offered to suspend all Kabuki plays in perpetuity.

Ernst's enlightened, methodical work might well have validated the Kabuki and countered the samurai-under-the-bed fears of the Occupation. However, the samurai-under-the-bed was soon succeeded by the Red-under-the-bed as the official phobia, and the occupiers came to see the feudal threat as much less pressing. Sometime after Ernst was transferred back to the United States and Bowers stepped into his place, the Kabuki was pronounced "liberated." The official American attitude was something like: "Sure, it might be a little feudal, but at least it isn't communist."

MOVIES

The Occupation's attitude toward the motion picture went through a similar, problematic transformation: from the search for fascist feudal remains to the great Red hunt. Here SCAP had a model to follow. Prewar and wartime Japanese cinema had been hedged with all sorts of rules and regulations, some of which were still useful to the Occupation. Although the CIE in 1945 had issued a memorandum concerning the elimination of Japanese government control of the motion picture industry, SCAP already had plans for its own censorship system, no less efficient and in some respects more so.

This subject and its results have been admirably studied by Kyoko Hirano.[13] Indeed, SCAP's treatment of cinema is, thanks to her scholarship, the single instance where one can in considerable depth observe the Occupation attitude toward artistic endeavor. There were enormities, including a big bonfire composed of the prints and negatives of films SCAP deemed "militaristic, ultra-nationalistic and feudalistic,"

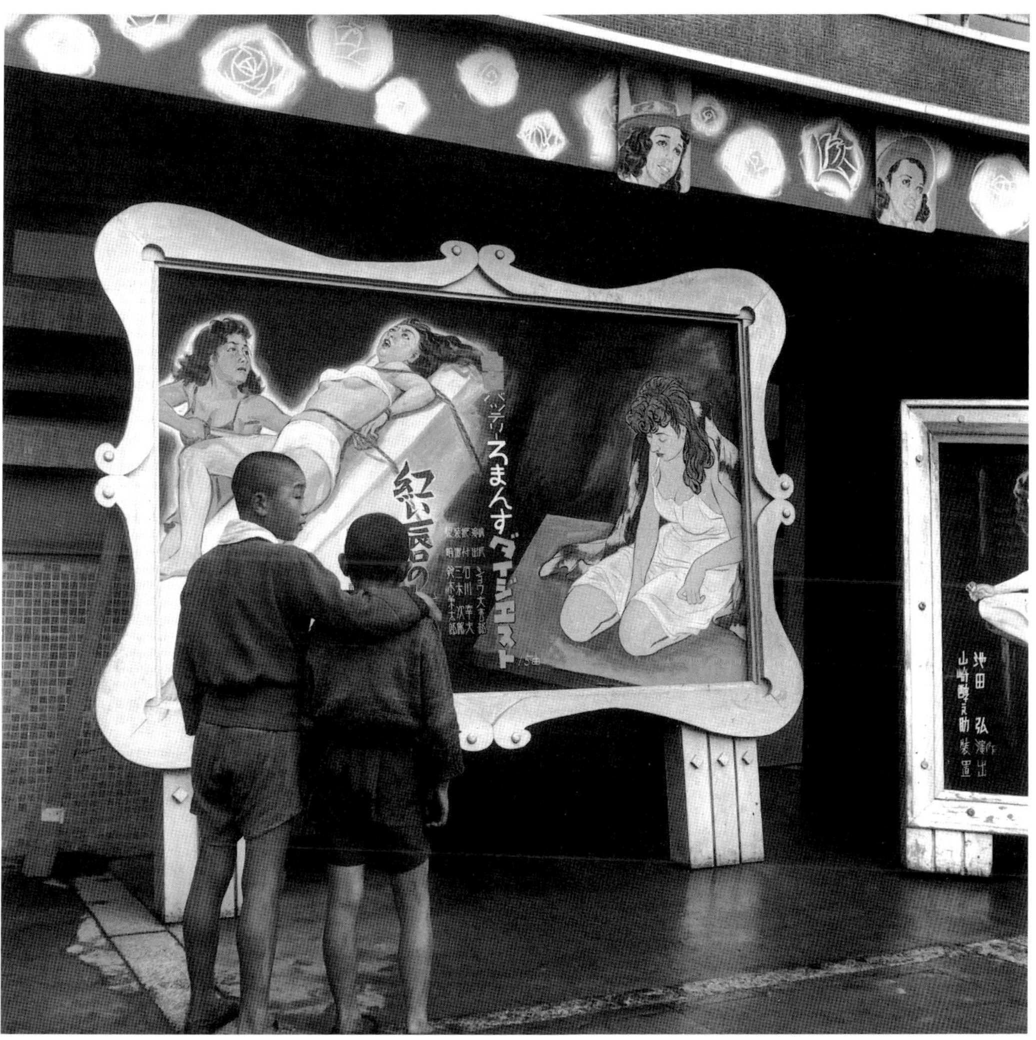

Horace Bristol, ***Two Little Boys Admiring Poster,*** **Tokyo, 1947. Black and white silver gelatin print.**

according to a memorandum to SCAP from the Japanese government's Central Liaison Office. There were also ironies: Kurosawa Akira's *They Who Step on the Tiger's Tail* (Tora no o o fumu otokotachi) was banned by the Japanese authorities as too democratic, then banned by the American authorities as too feudalistic, and had to wait until after the end of the Occupation for its release.

There were also the farcical elements never far from Occupation endeavor. Since the CIE covertly advocated kissing scenes as a symbol of moral liberation, there was a race among motion picture producers as to whose would be first. Since kissing had been strictly forbidden in wartime Japan (and routinely cut from all foreign films, much to the peril of their continuity), there was an amount of local discussion: Was it aesthetic? Was it hygienic? Was it Japanese? When it appeared that it was, the event was accomplished in 1946 in *Twenty-Year-Old Youth* (Hatachi no seishun).

SCAP's change of direction — from fascist-cleansing to communist-chasing — much complicated Occupation policy toward film. Though one of the policy's themes had initially been the presentation of an ideal America (anything less was unacceptable: all showings of *Citizen Kane* were strictly banned), the change from the image of a peace-loving, pacifist America to a cold war paranoid America was both sudden and extreme. As a result, some of the Occupation's most humane and liberal impulses remained unrealized.

This result was probably, if indirectly, to the benefit of artists. They were more likely to be left alone — unless, that is, their work was judged "communist." This was the case with *The Japanese Tragedy* (Nihon no higeki), a 1946 documentary by Kamei Fumio. It had been approved by both the CIE and the CCD, but was then suddenly banned by MacArthur himself. He did so at the personal request of General Charles Augustus Willoughby, head of military intelligence, who was in turn acting on the strong request of Premier Yoshida Shigeru. The premier, a political old-timer himself, had been enraged at what he considered a film too critical of Japan's wartime government. Providentially, Kamei was found to be a communist, and his work could thus be banned outright by the highest authority.[14] In such a manner were the original aims of the Occupation subverted and the later aims implemented.

A RETURN TO INDEPENDENCE

Nonetheless, with SCAP attention diverted from the question of what was or was not impermissibly feudal, it became possible for Japanese artists to return to their own themes and styles, achieving, though occupied, a degree of independence.

In fact, by the end of the Occupation in 1952, artists, writers, and filmmakers were far less curtailed than, for example, the average government worker busily engineering the "economic miracle." This degree of autonomy, this benign neglect of the arts, was also a legacy of the U.S. Occupation of Japan. ●

NOTES

1. Peter Frost, "Occupation," in *The Kodansha Encyclopedia of Japan* (Tokyo: Kodansha, 1983), 6:51.

2. Robert Spaulding, quoted in Thomas W. Burkman, ed., introduction to *The Occupation of Japan: Arts and Culture* (Norfolk, Va.: General Douglas MacArthur Foundation, 1988), p. vi.

3. Ikobe Makoto, ed., *The Occupation of Japan: U.S. Planning Documents* (Bethesda, Md.: Congressional Information Service, 1987).

4. David Waterhouse, "Japanese Art under the Occupation," in *Occupation of Japan: Arts and Culture,* p. 210.

5. Jacob Van Staaveren, in "Literature," panel discussion, ibid., p. 240.

6. *Occupation of Japan: Arts and Culture,* p. 177; and Meirion Harries and Susie Harries, *Sheathing the Sword* (New York: Macmillan, 1987), p. 185.

7. Theodore McNelly, in "The Impact of the Occupation on Literature," general discussion, in *Occupation of Japan: Arts and Culture,* p. 186.

8. Jay Rubin, in "Impact of the Occupation on Literature," ibid., p. 172.

9. Okuno Takeo, quoted by David Goodman in "Shingeki under the Occupation," discussion, ibid., p. 190.

10. J. Thomas Rimer, *Toward a Modern Japanese Theater* (Princeton, N.J.: Princeton University Press, 1974), p. 121.

11. Goodman, in "Shingeki," p. 190.

12. *Occupation of Japan: Arts and Culture,* p. 203.

13. Kyoko Hirano, "The Occupation and Japanese Cinema," ibid.

14. Kyoko Hirano, *Mr. Smith Goes to Tokyo: Japanese Cinema Under the American Occupation, 1945–1952* (Washington, D.C.: Smithsonian Institution Press, 1992), p. 133.

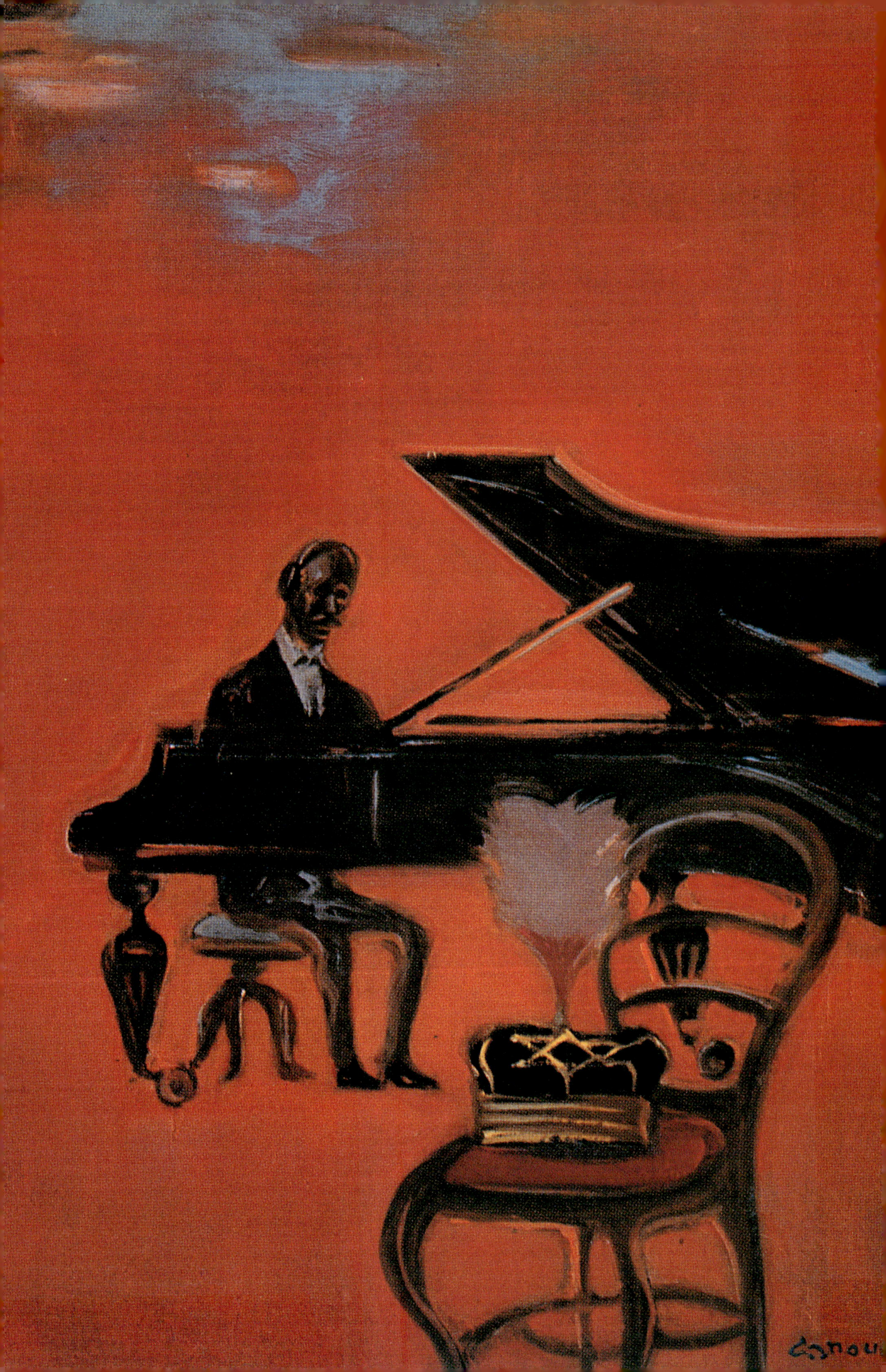

Painting in the Time of "Heavy Hands"

EMIKO YAMANASHI
EDITED BY J. THOMAS RIMER

Actually, the phrase "Occupation era" sounds a little odd to me, brought up as I was entirely in the postwar period. Japanese people usually call this time "confusion era" or "just after the war." The Occupation itself is a historical fact, yet in my Japanese history classes, the specifics were not taught clearly to us. For my generation, our responses are related rather to feelings associated with "the end of the war" or "the loss of the war." Apparently it is still difficult for the Japanese people to look at the period objectively. By extension, it is also difficult to gain true understanding of the art world between 1945 and 1952.

On August 15, 1945, when Japan surrendered, the so-called Great Japanese Empire was literally destroyed. With that destruction came the dissolution of the entire national system, including crucial government support mechanisms for culture and for the creation and display of contemporary painting. Faced with this collapse, artists were forced to accept a new situation and to ponder carefully what steps now might be taken.

Since the opening of Japan to the West at the beginning of the Meiji period (1868–1912), the government had become increasingly important in the world of art, and certainly in the war period of the 1930s and after, politicians had become even more conscious of the potential effect of the fine arts on society as a whole. Now, in 1945, these pressures were temporarily eliminated.

The significance of this change has its origins in recent history. When Japan opened its doors to the world in 1867 after virtually two hundred years of isolation, its leaders were eager for the country to internationalize and to show the world, and the Western nations in particular, that it was both a cultivated and a highly progressive nation. In the nineteenth century, international fairs and expositions provided a crucial mechanism that allowed government leaders to set forth a vision consonant with their ideas and hopes. From the Paris Exposition in 1867 onwards, Japan participated in virtually every important exhibition, including that of Chicago in 1893 and, again, Paris in 1900. Works of art were displayed in all these Japanese pavilions. Through those experiences, government officials learned that Japanese arts and crafts were well regarded by the citizens of Western nations who visited these fairs, and they learned that the international image of Japan was strongly influenced by the high quality of these works of art. It

Inoue Chozaburo, *Requiem*, 1949 (detail). See page 33.

was not surprising, then, that the government encouraged the teaching of painting, sculpture, and other arts.

In the field of painting, new ideas from Europe soon held sway, and young Japanese artists began experimenting with what they felt to be vibrant, exciting imported styles and methods. Even those who painted in more traditional ways began to absorb a wide variety of techniques from the West. Artists often banded together in groups reminiscent of the older traditional schools. Many included patrons and connoisseurs along with the artists themselves, and in the Meiji period it was not surprising that politicians also joined. In some cases, active encouragement by such officials spurred an interest in history painting, works that reflected a felt need on the part of politicians and government figures to emphasize the importance of Japanese history as a means to support the expanding roles of the national government and of the Emperor Meiji himself, who as a modern monarch now became a subject for the artist. By the turn of the century, the creation of contemporary art was increasingly sustained, and thus directed to some extent, by political considerations and the perceived needs of a national cultural system. Whatever cognizance individual artists may or may not have had of the prevalence of this system, they became increasingly subservient to it. National academies of painting, government-sponsored exhibitions (in some ways analogous to the Salon system in France), and other cultural institutions became more powerful.

Although the end of World War II did not, in the end, bring about the wholesale destruction of this national system, the Occupation years did provide a time in which its failures had to be examined realistically in order to bring about useful changes. Artists who, wittingly or unwittingly, had been concerned in their work with the fate of imperialism and nationalism were now forced to take stock.

Among the various discussions carried on at this time, one important issue concerned the "sincerity" of artists, and a second was couched in terms of an "argument for realism." Those who questioned the "sincerity" of artists during the war years castigated those painters who had served the government by creating war-related art, in hindsight seen to be propagandistic in nature, and now began to work again as though they had done nothing of which they should be ashamed. Fujita Tsuguji (1886–1968) was harshly criticized, for example. The spokesperson for those concerned with the true meaning of "realism" in art was Hijikata Teiichi, an influential art critic and later the director of the important Kanagawa Prefectural Museum of Modern Art in Kamakura. He maintained that in a deeper sense, the term "realism" refers not only to naturalistic representation. Rather, he insisted, the most important duty of artists is to capture what was truly real, expressing not only the visual surface but also a deeper reality as perceived in their minds and hearts. Hijikata remained critical of those artists who, during the war years, concerned themselves only with a realistic rendering on the surface of their paintings, as it were, yet shied away from seeing the deeper meaning of what they depicted. During the war period, he concluded, such "genuine" works might have been hard to create, but no such strictures could still be said to apply. Many artists, particularly those in the younger generation, took these words to heart and began to seek out new directions. Nevertheless, it took time for these new movements to develop.

Generally speaking, art developed in three streams during the 1940s and 1950s. Some artists' organizations simply reconstituted themselves. Other artists experimented with surrealism and abstraction, and energized by these new techniques, formed new, collegial artists' associations. A third group of artists remained independent, attempting to reflect with great seriousness on their personal experiences during the war.

ARTISTS' GROUPS

The first event to influence the first stream was the reorganization of the government art exhibition system. Discussions concerning such reorganization began within a month of the Japanese surrender. According to an article of September 10, 1945, in the influential newspaper *Mainichi,* the Imperial Committee on Fine Arts was already making plans to revive this system. "Today, since the rebuilding of Japanese art has become an important postwar issue, the means for re-creating governmental exhibitions has been discussed by the Ministry of Education. Members hope for a decision which will reflect the public interest."[1] A second article published on September 24 expressed the opinion that the activities of groups not associated with the government should also be encouraged. This viewpoint represented a considerable change from the prewar period.

Many, however, remained cautious. The art critic Ogawa Tekei, for example, wrote:

> **The most dangerous thing is an easy-going way of thinking based on an expectation grounded merely in optimistic feelings. Optimism without reason is more dangerous than a pessimism that always expects the worst. I believe that the kind of tough power needed to rebuild the world of the fine arts must exist within the context of an honest admission by artists who are able to state that "our works cannot be successful for a certain period of time, as we lost the war." I cannot believe that there are those who have the idea to simply revive governmental exhibitions by gathering its previous members [and then expect some progressive changes] just because the war has ended.**[2]

The only government-supported organization of art exhibitions that survived various contractions in the early 1940s was the so-called Teiten (Teitoku Bijutsu Tenraikai, Imperial Art Academy Exhibition). Now it was replaced by a new organization named Nitten (Nihon Bijutsu Tenraikai, Japan Art Exhibition), which held its first national exhibition in the spring of 1946. Such exhibitions were supported by the national budget; the juries were chosen by the Ministry of Education; and government policy directed them. Resisting the academism of governmental exhibitions proved to be a major impetus for organizations not associated with the government.

When the first Nitten exhibition opened, in the spring of 1946, however, there was a sense of fresh movement, as nongovernmental organizations were also invited

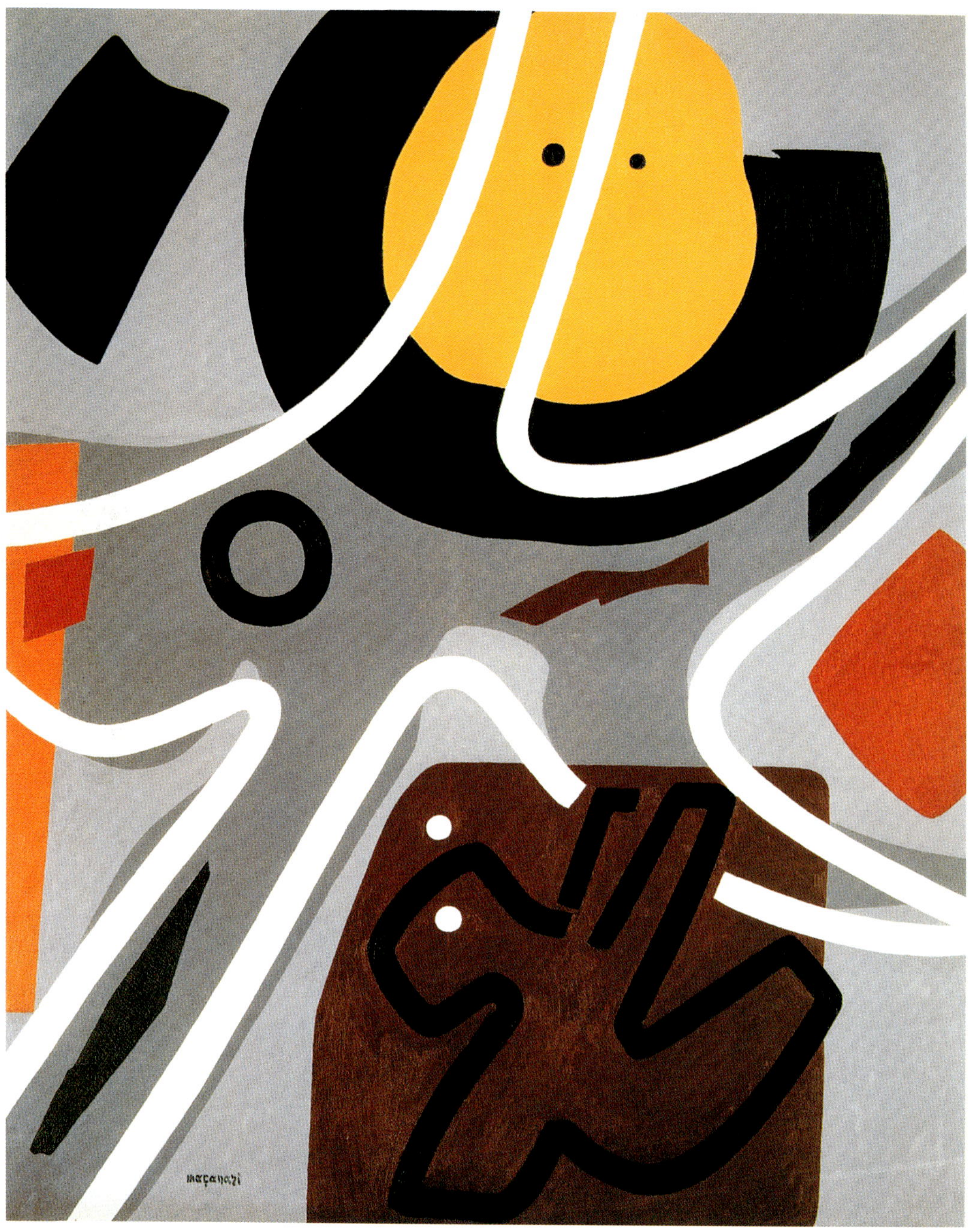

Figure 1. Murai Masanari, *Yellow Sun*, Japan, 1950. Oil on canvas, 161 x 130.5 cm. Tokyo Metropolitan Museum of Art

to participate. This new openness can certainly be seen as a tilt toward a more democratic approach. The independent and prestigious Nikakai Group (Second Division Group), to which a number of painters belonged, decided to take part, although certain painters who had originally joined Nikakai before the war because of its freedom from the restraints of the academic style were against joining. Such considerations induced a number of other influential organizations not to participate as well. The border between the academically included painters, whose artistic orientation had permitted affiliation with government groups during the war years, and the independent groups who had rejected such affiliations began to blur.

Nitten was not the only exhibition forum whose leanings Ogawa found so troubling. Immediately after Japan's surrender, on August 16, 1945, Togo Seiji, a prominent painter, met with a colleague named Takaoka Tokutaro to propose that, in these new circumstances, the Nikakai, an artist's organization to which both had once belonged but which had been forcibly disbanded during the war, should now reorganize as quickly as possible. The pair immediately began to contact former members. Painters who had suffered various restraints during the war were anxious to begin again, while those who had participated in the government-sponsored organizations were much slower to make decisions about their personal careers.[3]

Other groups, such as the Shin Seisaku Kyokai (New Creative Association), reflected in their own thinking the same conviction that, after the pressures of the wartime government against them, the surviving members should continue. The first postwar exhibition of their work was held in the autumn of 1946. Describing paintings by well-known artists Koiso Ryohei and Inokuma Gen-Ichiro, the art critic Yokokawa Kiichiro wrote: "Their works depict a nostalgia for France in a variety of compositions. These works delighted their viewers, since these artists express directly the freedom they have to enjoy European things again."[4] Yokokawa's analysis symbolizes the styles in which these artists worked.

Figure 2. Fukuda Toyoshiro, *Mary in Akita,* Japan, 1948. Color on paper, 180 x 223 cm. Akita Prefectural Museum

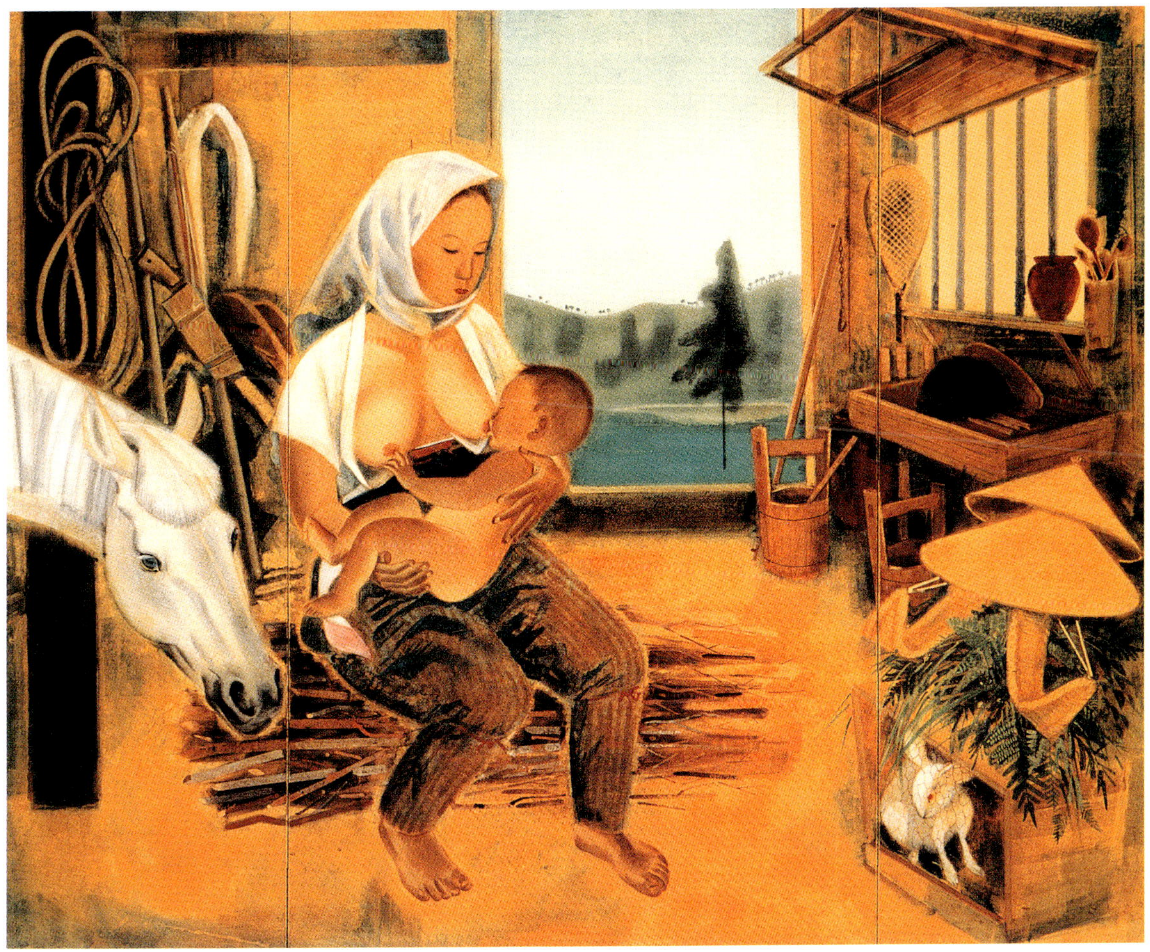

Other artists gravitated toward the second stream—the new experiments with surrealism and other avant-garde techniques, and they created an environment in which the ferment could take place. The painter Murai Masanari (born 1905), for example, headed a group of like-minded artists, who articulated his conviction, as well as that of other important painters such as Yamaguchi Kaoru, that they must work toward creating purely abstract paintings. Murai exhibited his famous *Yellow Sun* at the first exhibition by this group (fig. 1), saying it showed the sun not as white but as yellow, "since it burns."[5]

In 1948 artists working in the style of modern Japanese-style painting *(nihonga),* soon to become known as abstract painters, formed an artists' organization named Sozo Bijutsu (Creative Art), later renamed the Sogakai (Creative Painting Group). Among them were highly successful and admired artists such as Yamamoto Kyujin, Fukuda Toyoshiro (1904–1970), and Uemura Shoko. Their goal was to liberate

Figure 3. Mikami Makoto, *Mandala of F City,* Japan, 1950. Color on paper, 181.7 x 182 cm. Fukui Prefectural Museum of Art

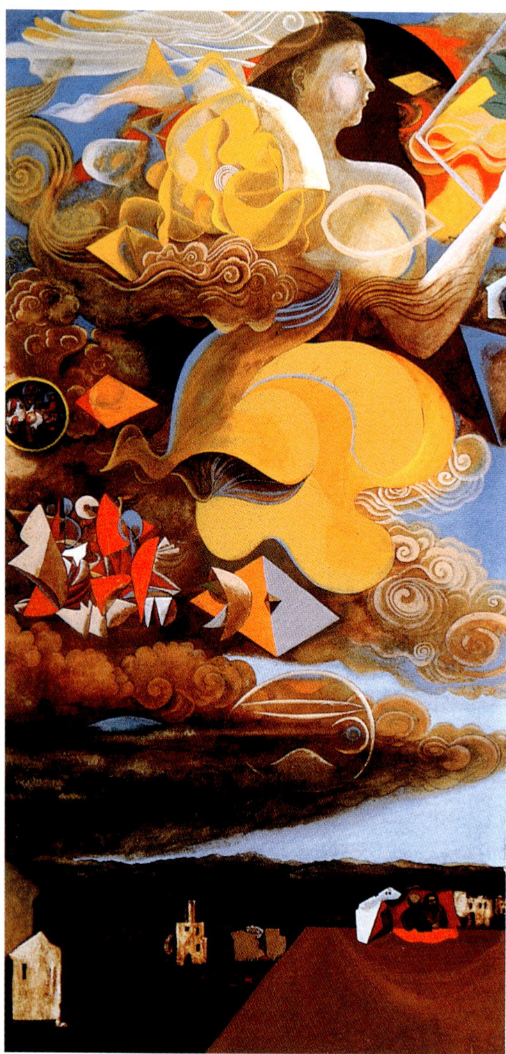

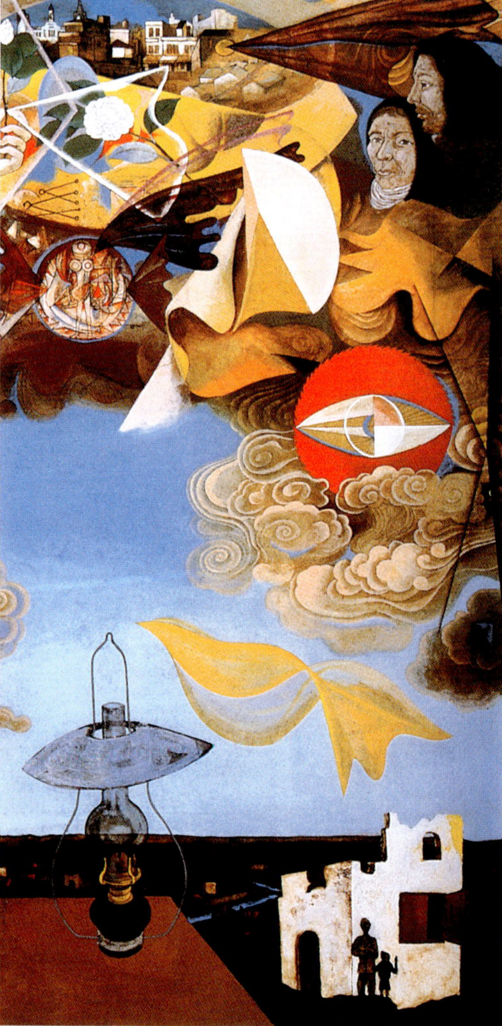

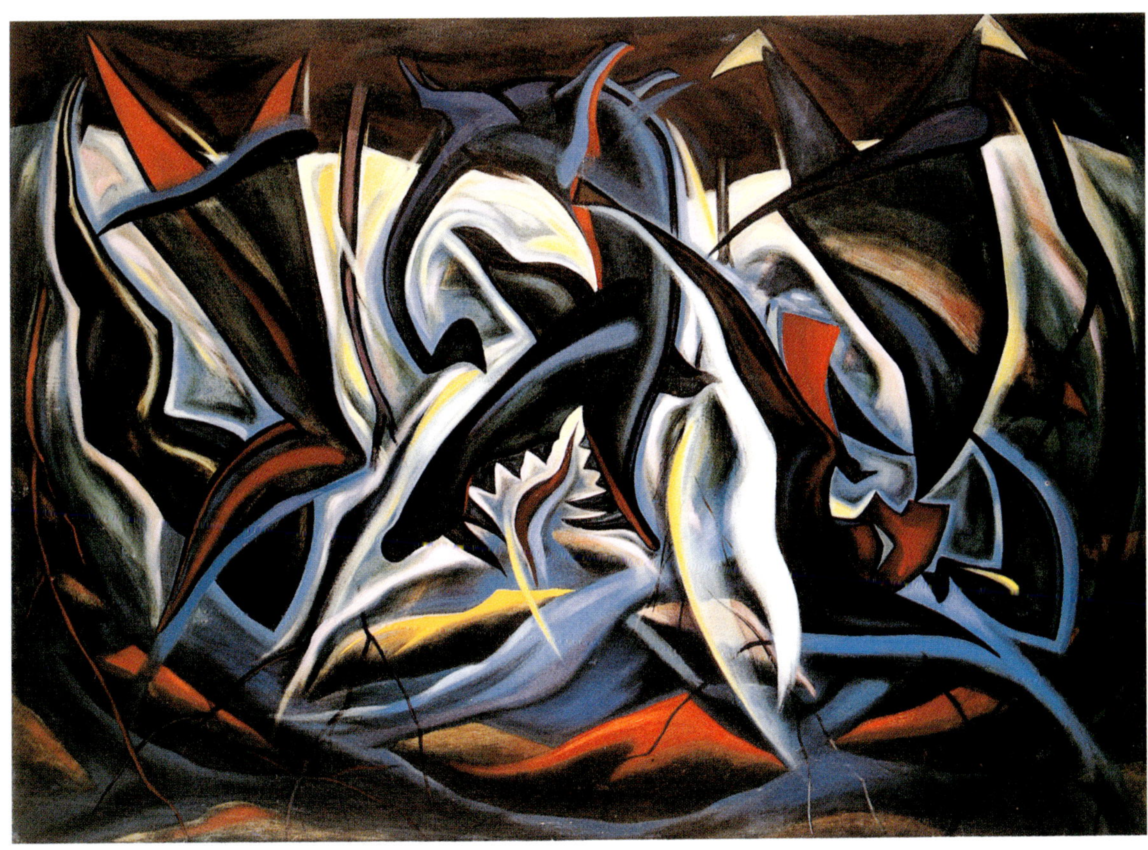

Figure 4. Okamoto Taro, *Dawn,* Japan, 1948. Oil on canvas, 181.7 x 256.5 cm. Tokyo National Museum of Modern Art

nihonga from an adherence to the traditionalism seemingly in disrepute after the war. Viewing this art as retrograde, these artists attempted to work in a thoroughly international style. Fukuda's *Mary in Akita* (fig. 2) was criticized because it was not *nihonga,* as it is strongly influenced by Paul Gauguin's works in Tahiti. Another important association, the Panriaru Bijutsu Kyôkai (Panreal Art Association), attempted to transcend what the members saw as the artificial barriers between Western-style painting *(yoga)* and *nihonga*. Typical of their work is *Mandala of F City* (fig. 3) by Mikami Makoto (1919–1972). Its title suggests the Buddhist background so often an element in older *nihonga* painting, but the subject matter — the bombing and burning of the painter's hometown, the city of Fukui — is rendered in a way that owes little to older decorative traditions.

Smaller groups played a crucial role as well. One group of artists and writers, calling themselves Yoru no Kai (Night Party), gathered around the talented painter Okamoto Taro (1911–1996). Their manifesto called for abandonment of materialism and sought to overcome the harsh realities of life at that juncture through artistic achievement. Okamoto's *Dawn* (fig. 4), for example, shown at the thirty-third Nikakai exhibition, attempted, in the artist's words, to express "all the complicated intercourse between the organic and the inorganic, the abstract and the representative, love and hate, beauty and ugliness, indeed all those juxtapositions that make extremely inharmonic sounds."[6]

Another such group, the Jikken Kobo (Experimental Atelier), had much in

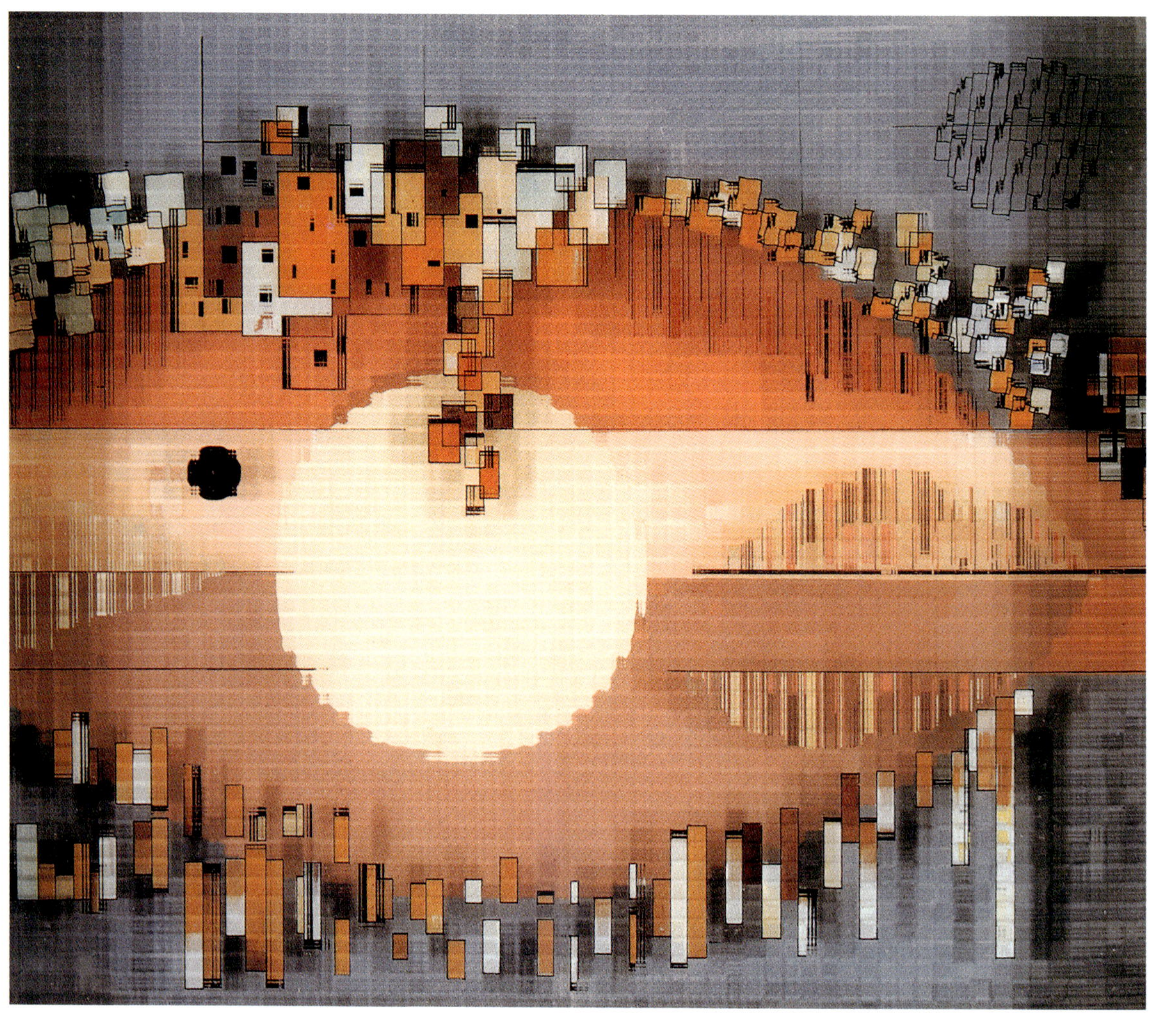

Figure 5. Yamaguchi Katsuhiro, *Vitrine*, Japan, 1952. Oil, watercolor, glass, wood, and paper, 56 x 65 cm. Tokyo Metropolitan Museum of Art

common with Yoru no Kai, for members included not only painters but also artists in other fields, ranging from music and literature to architecture and photography. Many of these artists combined diverse materials. The *Vitrine* of Yamaguchi Katsuhiro (born 1928), for example, is typical of their experiments, with a box of striped glass revealing an abstract painting behind it, arranged so that the visual image shifts depending on the viewer's angle of vision (fig. 5). The celebrated avant-garde poet Takiguchi Shuzo, then at the height of his influence as a writer and critic, was highly supportive of their activities.

INDEPENDENT ARTISTS

Works created by independent artists attempted to express war experiences directly. Many in this third stream depict a psychic landscape of the early postwar period. Kitawaki Noboru's (1901–1951) *Quo Vadis,* for example, portrays a man uncertain of the direction in which he should go: a long line of people stirs memories of lines of soldiers, or captives, while the blue of the sky suggests an infinite vacancy (fig. 6). In *Heavy Hands,* Tsuruoka Masao (1907–1979) suggests a state of psychic depression

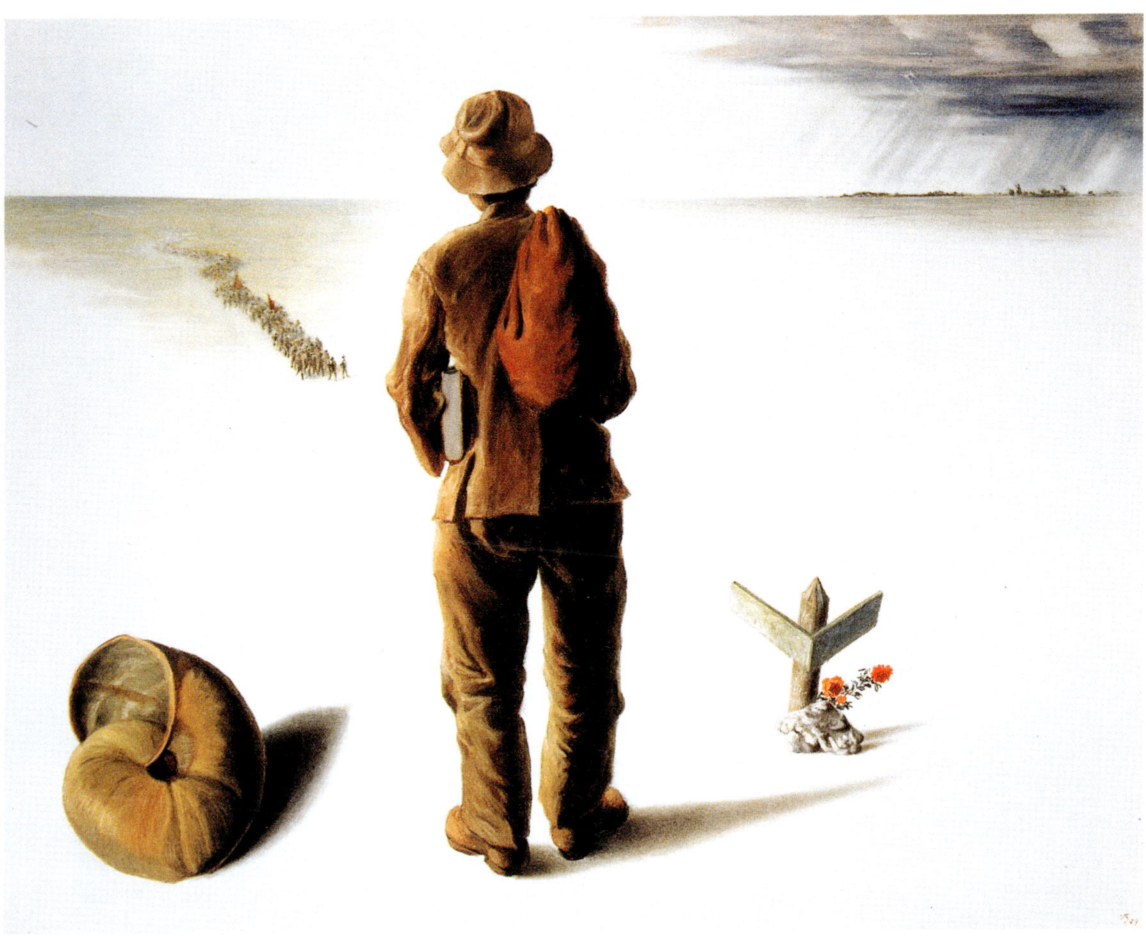

through his creation of figures with large and heavy hands (fig. 7). Inoue Chozaburo's (1906–1995) *Requiem* is unusual for its direct depiction of the political character of the person considered by many to be responsible for the war, for the man playing the piano is Tojo Hideki, prime minister when the hostilities broke out (fig. 8). In the painting, he wears headphones to allude to the time when he sat in the Tokyo War Crimes Trial, where he was eventually sentenced to death by hanging.

Figure 6. Kitawaki Noboru, *Quo Vadis,* Japan, 1949. Oil on canvas, 91 x 117 cm. Tokyo National Museum of Modern Art

One of the most notable painters to depict his war experiences is Kazuki Yasuo (1911–1974), whose work may be understood as typical of the way Japanese artists dealt with the war. Kazuki's career began like that of many other painters in the inter-war years. Born in 1911 in Yamaguchi Prefecture, at the southern tip of Honshu, the main island of Japan, he studied at the Tokyo School of Fine Arts, Japan's most prestigious training ground for modern artists. In the year of his graduation, his *Two Men Seated* (1936) was accepted for showing in the national government-sponsored exhibition, a considerable honor for such a young artist. Two years later, he took up work as a high school teacher in his home prefecture and continued his own artistic work.

In 1943, however, Kazuki's career took quite an unexpected turn. Drafted into the army, he was sent to northern China, where, at that time, the situation remained relatively quiet. Those in charge of his military unit, aware of his talent, allowed him to continue his art during his spare time. While he was in China he sent some 350 postcards to his family in Japan on which he made various sketches. From time to time he indicated that he was working on some paintings on his own or had been commissioned to do others. He even completed a work that he sent all the way from China to the major annual national government-sponsored exhibition, and he was able to keep up his connections with Fukushima Shigetaro, then well known as an art dealer and critic. Kazuki's last postcard from China was sent in June 1945.

Figure 7. Tsuruoka Masao, *Heavy Hands,* Japan, 1949. Oil on canvas, 130 x 97 cm. Tokyo Metropolitan Museum of Art

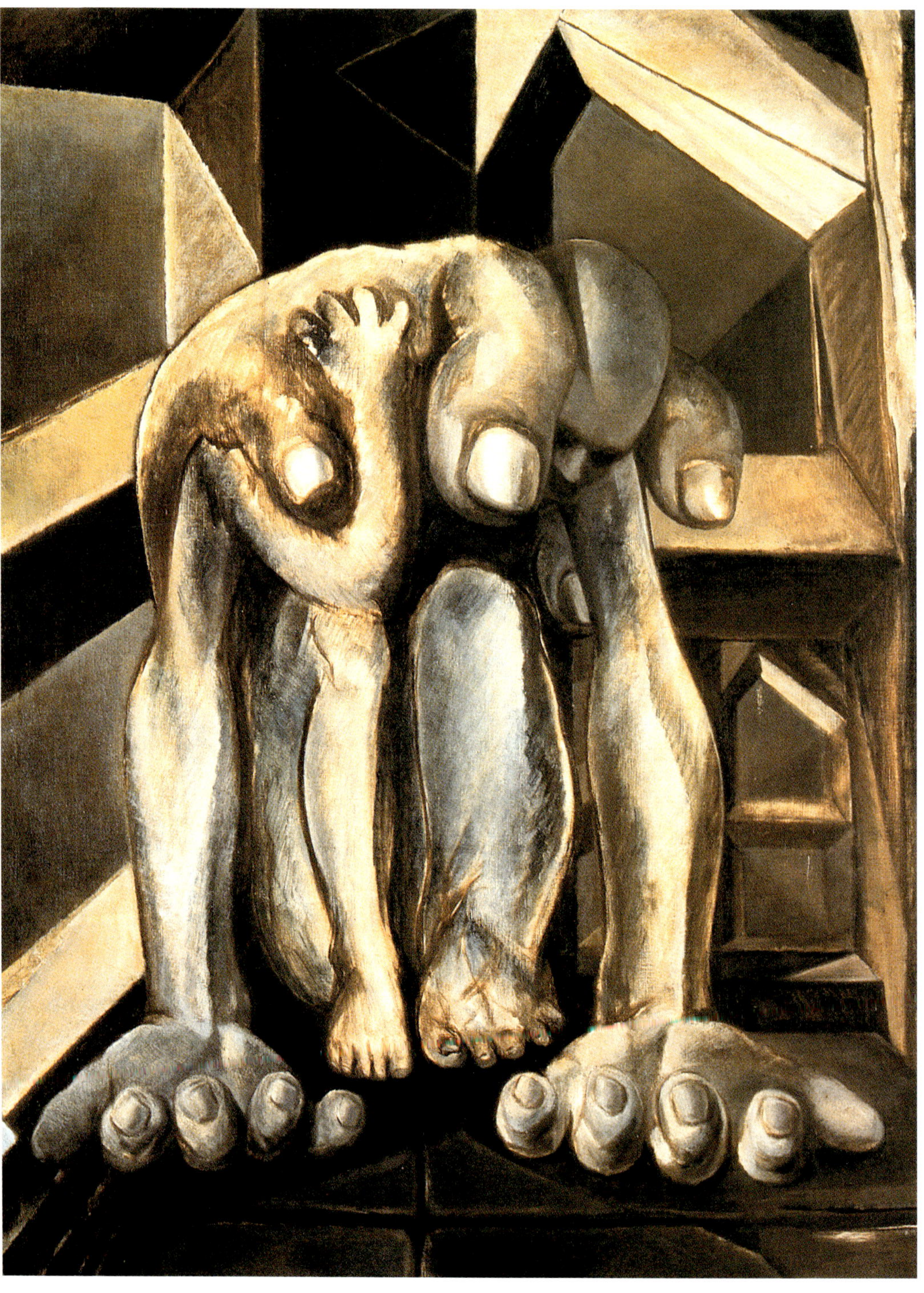

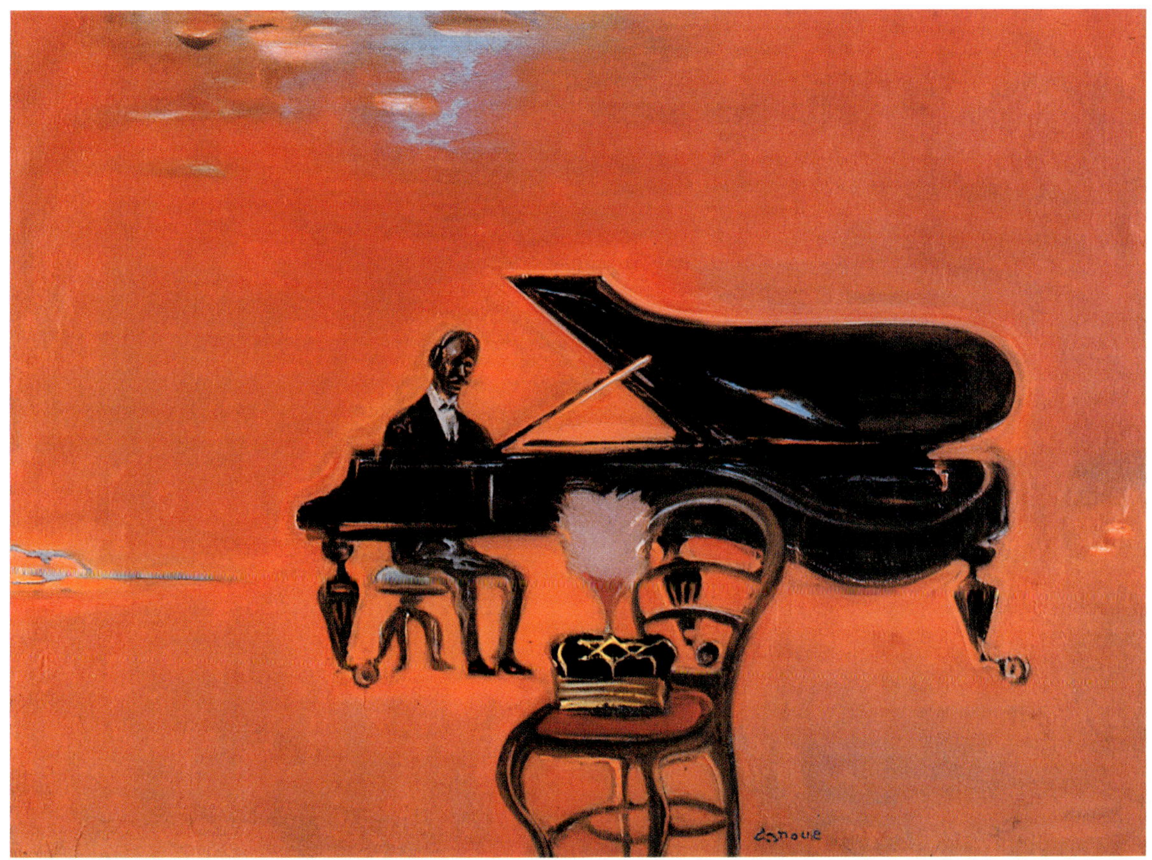

Figure 8. Inoue Chozaburo, *Requiem*, Japan, 1949. Oil on canvas, 97.3 x 130.5 cm. Iwaki Municipal Museum of Art

When the war ended, Kazuki was still in China, but as he and another group of soldiers were attempting to leave, they were captured by Soviet soldiers and eventually removed to Siberia. During the winter months, when the temperature dropped as low as minus 40 degrees centigrade, the painter and the others in his group were confined in a rough cabin, with only wood panels for beds and one thin blanket for cover. In this harsh environment, many of the Japanese prisoners died. For food the prisoners were only given a small amount of a white flour-like substance, which each would mix with snow and bake on the stove.

In addition, the prisoners were assigned hard physical tasks to perform. One of the survivors later said that, in their physical state, it would take several hours to cut down a tree of only one meter in diameter; if the tree were two meters, it would take them up to two days. Since they were given one extra cup of flour if they could surpass the usual goals, some tried to work much harder, literally straining themselves to death. Under these conditions it is hard to imagine that Kazuki could continue his artistic work in any way. Yet he had enough presence of mind to use his talents for self-preservation, drawing some naked female figures for the Russian soldiers in exchange for food.

In 1946 the Japanese prisoners were transported to Chernyakhovsk, where daily life became a bit better. Each prisoner was quizzed as to his special skills. When Kazuki mentioned that he was a painter, he was assigned the task of creating posters and

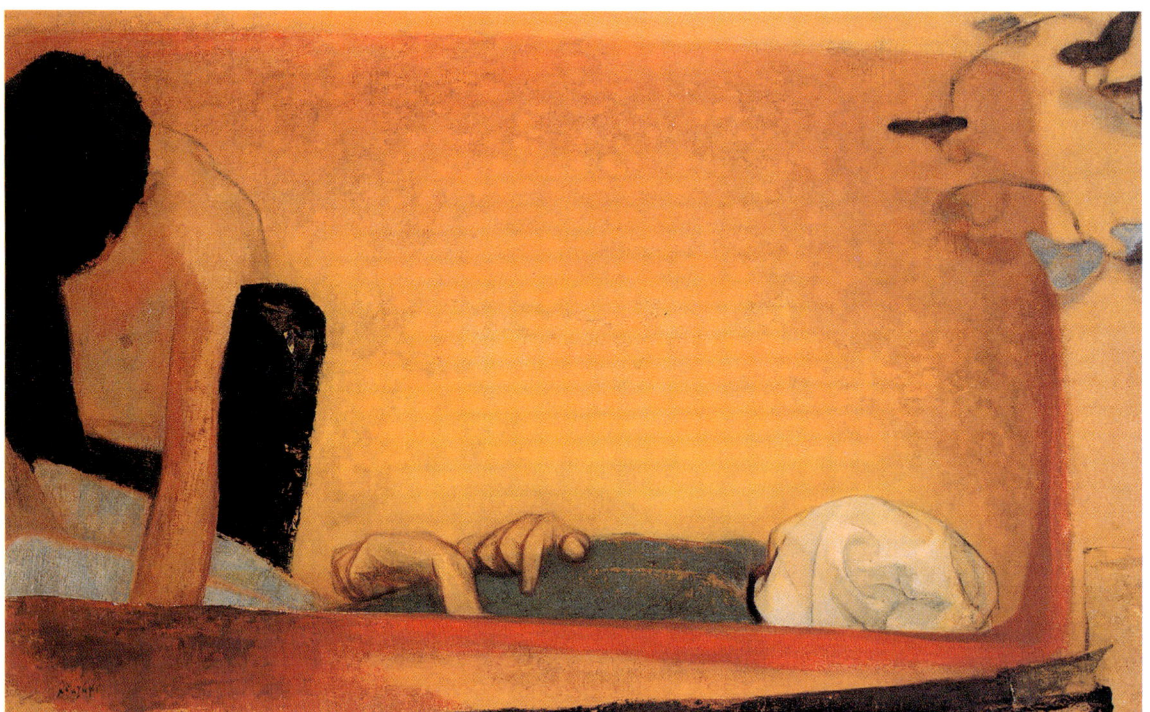

Figure 9. Kazuki Yasuo, *Burial,* Japan, 1948. Oil on canvas, 72.2 x 117.1 cm. Private collection

some portraits. Although he found himself delighted to be asked to work as an artist, he was unsatisfied, as such work was not, for him, truly creative in nature. Seeking a means of self-expression, he chose twelve subjects for future works and wrote their titles on the back of his painting box. The so-called Siberia series he later created make use of these subjects. The first of them, *Burial,* was painted in 1948, the year after he was repatriated to Japan (fig. 9). Kazuki later wrote:

> **I made a decision to create this composition when I was a prisoner. The painting was created not long after I returned home. It is the first work in my "Siberia series," and, after finishing it, I could not for a time work on any more subjects based on my experiences there, since I needed to fix the meaning of those years in my own mind. For this reason, *Burial* looks rather different from the other works in the series, as it uses bright colors. I had consciously chosen to paint with bright colors for several years after I returned home, perhaps because I wanted to find a way to tell myself that this dark period of my life was now gone by. And I certainly wanted to depict the burial of my friends during the war in the warmest way possible.**[7]

Of the works in this Siberia series, only the first was painted in the Occupation era. The other works Kazuki painted around 1950 depict nothing directly related to the war. But late in the decade he returned to the Siberia series. As a work like *To the North, To the West* shows, the artist was now to concentrate on a limited palette of dark colors, often black and ocher (fig. 10). Of this picture, Kazuki wrote that when the train, packed with Japanese prisoners, left northern China in September 1945,

Figure 10. Kazuki Yasuo, *To the North, To the West,* Japan, 1959. Oil on canvas, 72.9 x 116.7 cm. Yamaguchi Prefectural Museum of Art

"we did not know where we were being sent; so we tried to look through the window of the train, hoping that we were to be returned home. Even in despair, we were still eager to know where we were going."[8]

The same hands, the same faces appear over and over again in the Siberia series. Although Kazuki explored other subjects until his death in 1974, he continued to create additional works in this series. The depth of his reactions to his experience can be seen, first in an initial decade of silence, then in the series' long continuation.

Kazuki's ten years of silence exemplifies how Japanese artists continued to struggle to accommodate their wartime experiences. In trying to grasp the attitudes prevalent in those difficult years, it is useful to recall critic Sawachi Hisae's analysis of a book entitled *The Glory of a Homeless Boy*. Its author, Sano Mitsuo, lost his whole family during the war and became homeless at the age of twelve. After a difficult, miserable period, he eventually began to write stories for children. *The Glory of a Homeless Boy,* which served as a kind of autobiography, was therefore an unusual work for him. In fact, only a thousand copies were printed, and the book never reached a second edition. In a postscript, Sano wrote that:

> **In my view, to publish a book in order to demonstrate some denial of war is a hateful thing. If someone comes to hate war just because of reading a book, then one might support wars after reading something else. A true hatred for war must constitute a faith that lies deep in the individual human heart. It should not be shaken so easily, one way or the other.**[9]

Later Sano observed:

I think each one of us knows that there are those who, although they may say nothing, hate war more than those who scream against it. They scream, but they are being used by politics, and their voices do not sound from the bottom of their hearts. I am against all wars, but not because I lost my whole family in World War II. Nor did I express such a passive acceptance in *The Glory of a Homeless Boy*. And, if I had, I suppose the book would have sold more copies. That war was not begun by anyone other than the Japanese people themselves, and all of my family members, including myself as a child, felt positive about that war.[10]

Quoting these lines, Sawachi concludes that Sano's solution, rather than writing about his own life, was to write literature for the children of future generations. His response to his experience in war is not unlike Kazuki's or that of other artists whose memories were painful. Many artists and writers could not live by selling the secrets of their souls, seared through their own harsh experiences. Sano understood such a reaction, and his words show great sympathy for those who tried to move ahead. ●

NOTES

1. "Bunten saiken e ippo, myoshun 3-gatsu kaisai ka, chujun Teikoku Geijutsuin Dai 1-bukai- (Approach to reviving Bunten exhibition possibly next March: Imperial Academy of Art Dept. 1 meets in the mddle of this month) *Mainichi* newspaper, September 10, 1945, cited in Masanobu Hosono, "Soron" (General remarks), in *Nitten shi* (History of Nitten), (Tokyo: Nitten, 1980–88), vol. 16.

2. Ogawa Tekei in *Bijutsu,* November 1945, cited in ibid.

3. Taki Teizo. "Nika 70-nenshi (Seventy-year history of Nika) in *Nika nanajunenshi,* ed. Nika Nanajunenshi Henshu Iinkai (Editorial Committee of Seventy-year history of Nika) (Tokyo: Nikkei Jigyo Shuppansha, 1985), p. 6.

4. Takeda Michitaro. "Shinseisaku Kyokai 50-nen gaishi" (Fifty-year history of Shinsesaku Kyokai), in *Shinseisaku gojunen* (Fifty years of Shinseisaku), ed. Shinseisaku Kyokai 50-nenshi Hensan Iinkai (Editorial Committe of Fifty-year history of Shinsesaku Kyokai) (Tokyo: Shinseisaku Kyokai, 1986), p.151.

5. Miki Tetsuo "Comments on *Kiiroi Taiyo* (Yellow sun), by Murai Masanari," in Hotla Shinya, ed. *Showa no bijutsu* (Art from the Showa period). Vol. 3: 1946–1955, p. 86. Tokyo: Mainichi Shinbusha, 1990–91.

6. Tanaka Atsushi, "Comments on *Yoake* (Dawn), by Okamoto Taro," ibid., p. 71.

7. Kazuki Yasuo, "Comments on *Maiso* (Burial), by Kazuki Yasuo," in Kazuki Yasuo, *Kazuki Yasuo: Shiberiya Shirizu* (Kazuki Yasuo exhibition: series Siberia) (Kofu City: Yamanashi Prefectural Museum of Art, 1995), p. 42.

8. Iwata Rei, *Kazuki Yasuo* (Tokyo: Nichido Shuppan, 1977).

9. Sano Mitsuo, "Furoji no eiko" (Glory of a homeless boy) (1961), cited in Sawachi Hisae, *Senkyuhyaku-yonjunen no shojo* (A girl in 1945) (Tokyo: Bungei Shunju, 1982), p. 97.

10. Ibid., p. 99.

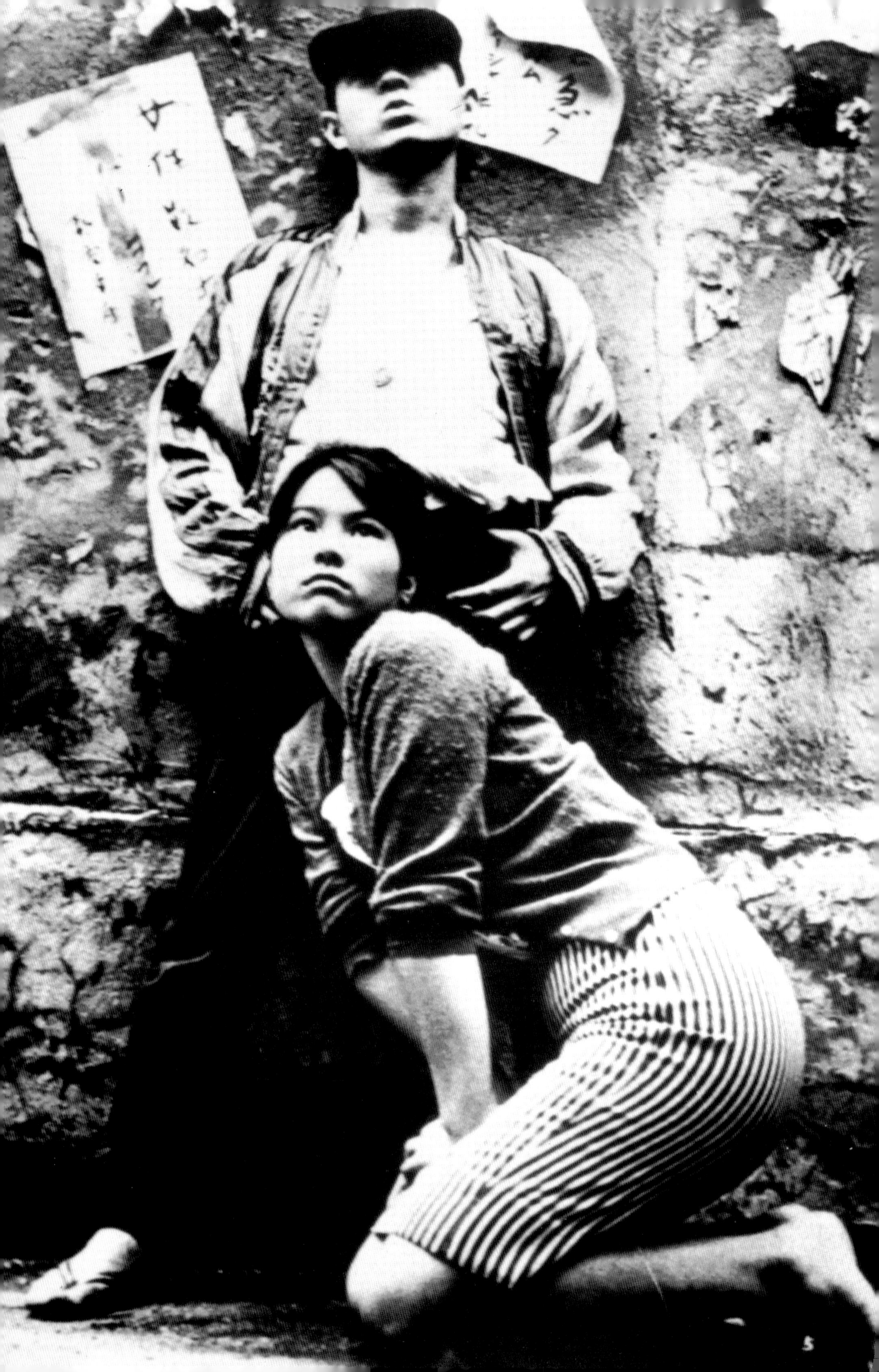

Erasing and Refocusing: Two Films of the Occupation

LINDA C. EHRLICH

The big screen grants the filmmaker surprising power to create history — as anyone who has seen the works of Oliver Stone can attest: historians may waver, but millions of moviegoers have been convinced beyond doubt that John F. Kennedy was assassinated by a conspiracy and that Richard M. Nixon was an alcoholic. A sketchy theory, when fleshed out with all the visual and aural effects at the filmmaker's disposal, can take on the certainty of fact, and the project of presenting history through film can be a dubious one.

Yet these same means can also deepen viewers' understanding. Films by two of Japan's greatest living directors, Shinoda Masahiro's 1984 *MacArthur's Children* (Setouchi shonen yakyudan) and Imamura Shohei's 1961 *Pigs and Battleships* (Buta to gunkan), express distinctively Japanese views of the Allied Occupation. They are among the few Japanese films on this era that are accessible outside Japan, and both offer alternative interpretations of a period that has often been presented, too simplistically, as a tribute to "democratization" and "progress."[1]

Shinoda's *MacArthur's Children* is a lyrical, almost nostalgic presentation of the Occupation as a period of hardship yet opportunity; Imamura's *Pigs and Battleships,* based on a novel by Otsuka Kazu, offers a rawer look at a time of opportunity and exploitation. Despite their differences, the two films grapple seriously with historical realities, and each offers a Japanese view of Japanese behavior during the Occupation in which the Americans involved are seen mainly as a backdrop.

DIRECTORIAL VISION

Early in their careers, both Imamura (born 1926) and Shinoda (born 1931) worked as assistants to a giant of the classical Japanese film, Ozu Yasujiro, but each diverged from Ozu's vision. Although both could be classified as New Wave directors, their paths have not been parallel. Like the other directors of Japan's New Wave in the 1960s, who originally rebelled against the older studio system, they identified themselves with Japan's youth culture and against political developments like the renewal of the Treaty of Mutual Cooperation and

Kinta, the gangster wannabe, and his girlfriend Haruko, in *Hogs and Warships* (also known as *Pigs and Battleships*). She is an early example in a series of resilient women seen in Imamura's films.

Figure 1. The Japan-American All-Star Game, from *MacArthur's Children.* Baseball serves as a leitmotif in the film, a metaphor for the linked destinies of Japan and the United States.

Security in 1960. But while Shinoda has moved back and forth between an explicitly theatrical style and a softer historicism, Imamura tends to depict lower levels of society — prostitutes, pimps, B-grade actors, local mafia. Frequently relying on metaphors from nature, including bestial ones, Imamura's films, including *The Insect Woman* (Nippon konchuki, 1963) and *The Pornographers* (Jinruigaku nyumon, 1966), are often bluntly realistic, almost documentary. He provides us with a view of what one French critic has aptly described as "the vital, primitive, illogical and contradictory energy of the authentic Japan."[2] More recently, however, Imamura returned, in part, to an Ozu-like style in *Black Rain* (Kuroi ame, 1989), with its restrained treatment of the effects of radiation stemming from the Hiroshima bombing.

The typical quickness of Imamura's editing, resembling that of his compatriot Kurosawa Akira, contrasts with Shinoda's style, which often follows a more elegant rhythm. In films like *Demon Pond* (Yashagaike, 1980) and *Gonza the Spearman* (Yari no Gonza, 1987), Shinoda presents a kind of detached beauty in the face of harsh realities, drawing on traditional stylistics from the Kabuki and Bunraku (puppet) theater. His *gendaigeki* (contemporary drama) films and his documentaries share this heightened aestheticism and depict the ephemerality of life while also pointing to the underlying darker, often erotic forces in Japanese society.[3]

MacArthur's Children lacks the daring mix of historical narrative and avant-garde set and music found in earlier Shinoda films, such as *Double Suicide* (Shinju ten no Amijima, 1969). It opens with the emperor's radio announcement on August 15 that Japan had lost the war. Documentary footage of General Douglas MacArthur's entry into Japan is mixed with shots of the Genbaku Domu (Atomic Bomb Dome) in Hiroshima; schoolchildren grind ink to obliterate any reference in their textbooks to the glories of Japan's wartime prowess.

Covering such serious themes with a disarmingly light tone, Shinoda presents an Occupation period in which war crimes trials and executions are mixed with baseball tournaments and the semicomical loss of precious black-market rice. Underneath this deceptively smooth surface, however, *MacArthur's Children* stresses the essential role of the inner strength of the Japanese people in making the Occupation a success — a strength that triumphs over material concerns. Shinoda's characters overcome obstacles with resilience and resourcefulness. And, through the role of the war criminal (played with appropriate restraint by actor-turned-director Itami Juzo), Shinoda vividly depicts the grief that the war crimes trials caused to the Japanese.

In *Pigs and Battleships,* by contrast, Imamura criticizes not only the U.S. military bases still in Japan, which he considers a necessary evil, but also those Japanese who become so obsessed after the war by material gain and by an attachment to old ideologies that they lose the ability to think clearly and to lead independent lives. *Pigs and Battleships* shows how quickly the dreams of youth can be tarnished in a rapidly changing society. In both films, the overstated performances by some of the more comic characters add a destabilizing sense of celebrating among the ashes.

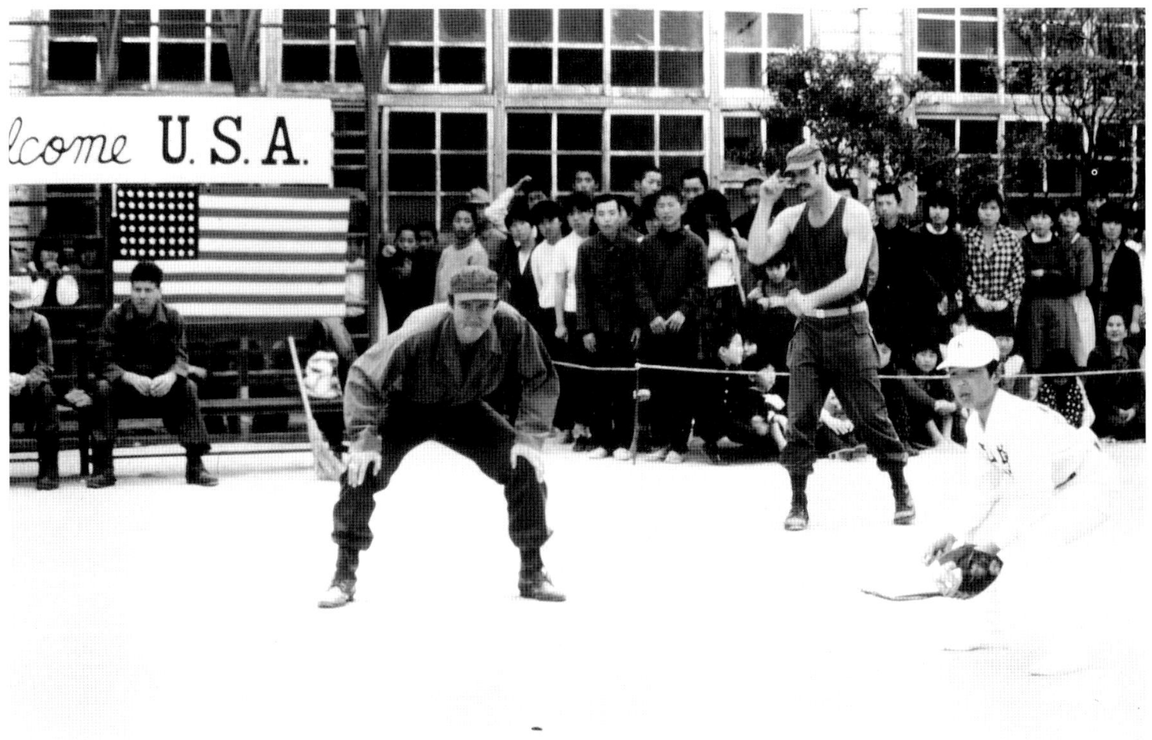

OPENINGS

Both films begin with a mixture of festive notes and darker undertones. The opening of *Pigs and Battleships* features "Stars and Stripes Forever" on the soundtrack. Yet the accompanying visual scene immediately establishes the film's sardonic mood: drunken American servicemen solicit and / or are accosted by Japanese prostitutes in a bawdy red-light district near the Yokosuka Naval Base. Imamura fills this sequence with high-angle shots that reduce the people to the size of insects, thus providing a clue that their grandiose plans are doomed to failure.

Shinoda begins *MacArthur's Children* with the upbeat "In the Mood" melody over red, white, and blue titles — but also over scenes of Hiroshima, homelessness, and war wounded. This sequence gives way to a mixture of staged and documentary footage of the dignified, sometimes tearful reaction of the Japanese to the emperor's radio announcement. Together, the sound and visuals set the tone of that film: a bittersweet recollection of a time just beyond the horrors of war that seemed to offer the promise of better things to come.

BASEBALL

Although baseball would seem to represent a quintessentially Western import imposed on post-World War II Japan, in *MacArthur's Children* it serves as an apt metaphor for the interconnected destinies of Japan and the United States (fig. 1). Shinoda emphasizes that it was a solidly Japanese sport by making one of the film's

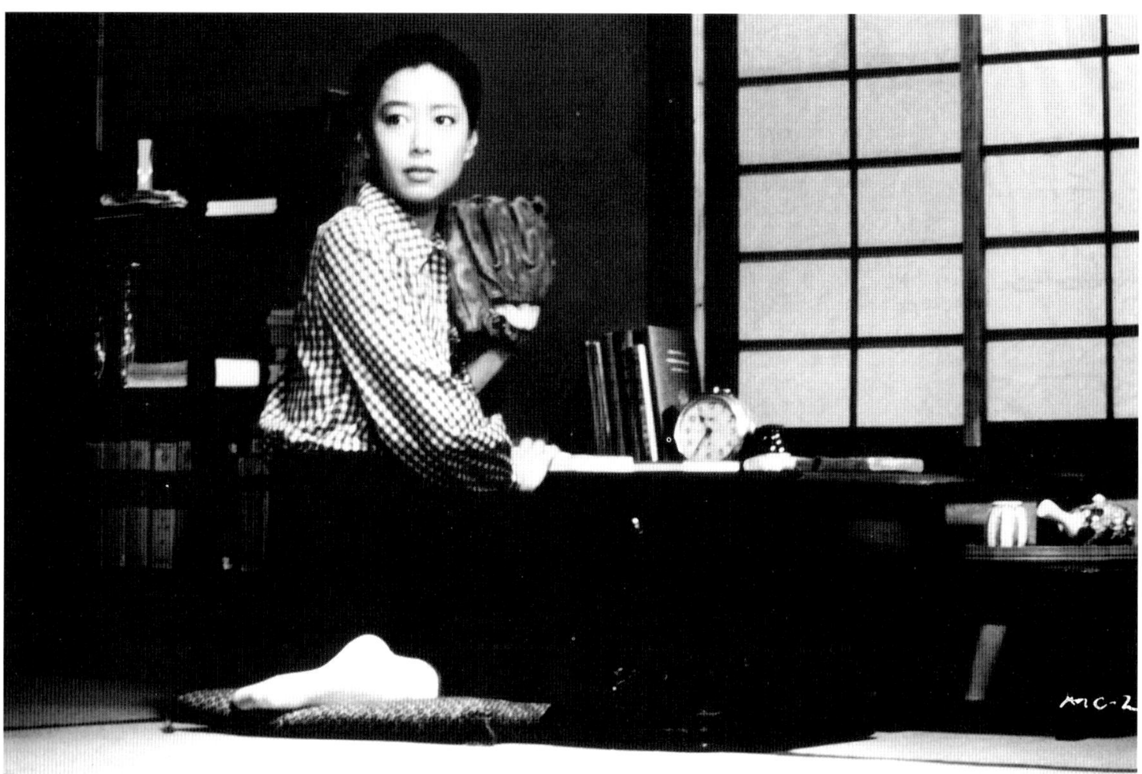

Figure 2. The schoolteacher Komako, who uses baseball to motivate students disoriented by the results of Japan's wartime defeat, is the moral center of Shinoda's film.

Japanese protagonists, Masao (played by the popular singer and actor Go Hiromi), a former baseball player — a star in the 1930s — who lost a leg as a soldier in the war. The film's title translates literally as "Setouchi Boys' Baseball Team," and indeed baseball becomes the leitmotif of the film, linking past, present, and future among the Japanese. It exemplifies the merging of Western technology and Japanese spirit that Japanese authorities had been espousing since the mid-1800s.

The past is invoked when the Japanese spectators at the concluding baseball game beat on traditional drums, as if participating in an annual harvest dance, to inspire their team. Baseball's role in the present figures in the desire of the elementary school teacher Komako (Natsume Masako) to motivate her motley class of students, disoriented by the changes brought on by military defeat (fig. 2). And as the team progresses from the ridiculous to the exemplary, Masao, the deeply depressed veteran of a lost battle, regains his confidence on the sidelines as a coach. It is only through baseball that the defeated Masao can find a path for himself away from injury, toward the possibility of a new career in the future. Shinoda has described his own view of the Japan-American All-Star Game that concludes his film:

> **The children playing baseball with the American soldiers in the film has nothing to do with revenge. It was not the Americans who killed the father [the war criminal], but rather it was we who were responsible for his execution. Back then, we thought that we were to be blamed and not our enemy, and I still think so now.**[4]

Despite Shinoda's assertion that there is no revenge motivating the ball game between the Japanese schoolchildren and the American servicemen, the game includes a reference to the soul of the war criminal "returning" in the form of a dog that unexpectedly appears and grabs the ball in its mouth, thus allowing the Japanese children to emerge triumphant. It would be hard to imagine the generally celebratory finale of the film had the Americans won. What the baseball game represents is a progression of three generations of Japanese (grandparents, teachers, and children) through bitter memory on to a spiritual, if not military, victory.

In contrast to the upbeat baseball theme in Shinoda's film, Imamura prefers to concentrate on more adult games. While the poverty endured by the Japanese after the war is presented only obliquely by Shinoda, Imamura reminds his viewers over and over that, in a country defeated militarily and economically, money and merchandising are everything. Only in rare moments does Imamura evoke a past glory, as when the gaze of a drunken, dispirited man pans up to a photograph of a young and eager Japanese soldier displayed on his wall. As for baseball, Imamura's only shot of the game shows postwar Japanese children playing it in the rubble of a housing project.

GANGSTERS

Although the gangster theme seems to be a connecting thread between both films, Shinoda offers a lighter satirical view than does Imamura, in keeping with the general approach in *MacArthur's Children* of accepting difference and moving on. One of the schoolboys in *MacArthur's Children,* Saburo (Omori Yoshiyuki), longs to become a *baraketsu* (a slang word for "gangster"), and he eventually quits school to join two older characters, whom he calls his "brother and sister," in black market activities. These two, with their flashy clothing and uncouth manners, are drawn directly from American gangster films. As in Shinoda's *Pale Flower* (Kawaita hana, 1963), the ceremonial behavior found among gangsters is portrayed with a note of irony.

The stakes seem higher for the gangster-wannabe Kinta (Nagato Hiroyuki) in *Pigs and Battleships* (fig. 3). A Japanese James Dean type, he tries to fit into a group of older *yakuza* (gangsters) whose activities are more sinister than the cartoonlike gangster and moll in Shinoda's film. Imamura's gangsters rough people up for money and dump dead bodies into the ocean. Kinta trails after them slavishly — like an older variant of the gullible schoolboy Saburo in *MacArthur's Children.* In *Pigs and Battleships,* the gangsters represent the tough new breed of Japanese who manipulate the general societal instability of the time to their own advantage.

These two characters' disappointment with the gang "family" offers a telling contrast between the two films: the moment of disillusionment proves a bittersweet turning point for Saburo, but a fatal mistake for Kinta. The codes of loyalty to the group associated even with an illegal entity like the *yakuza* are shown in *Pigs and Battleships* to be merely a thin veneer covering up laziness and the desire for quick financial gain. The metaphorical use of pigs is apt. By the end of the film, in which porcine behavior abounds, those animals, subverting the usual Japanese reverence for cleanliness, can no longer be contained.

DEMOCRACY AND AMERICANIZATION

Two weeks after the emperor's speech admitting defeat, armadas of American forces began to arrive in Japan. What followed was a time when General MacArthur, the "shadow shogun," attempted to destroy the Japanese war machine, dismantle the *zaibatsu* (the domination of Japanese finance, commerce, and industry by a few families), and carry out land reform. Meanwhile the Japanese also moved forward on their own agenda, aimed at such goals as the formation of a government-guided economy. The meeting of cultures went far beyond chewing gum, nylons, "kissing scenes" in movies, and songs like "You Are My Sunshine," whistled by GIs.

This was a time when enthusiasm for democracy was everywhere, but no one — including the Americans — was sure what it would mean for the Japanese. Shinoda cleverly points up this uncertainty in a scene in which the schoolboy Ryuta (Yamauchi Kaya) anxiously responds to the new injunction for coed classrooms with the question: "Is that democracy?" Later, the self-reliant war widow Tome (played by Shinoda's wife, Iwashita Shima) angrily asserts that "women are equal now" but finds her barbershop-turned-bar closed down as business moves away to larger cities like Osaka and Tokyo.

In *Pigs and Battleships,* one gang member rationalizes that because democracy means a move away from feudal-period hierarchies, stealing pigs from their leader is a way of "democratizing" the gang. These gangsters (who beneath their tough exteriors are actually cowards and hypochondriacs) espouse loyalty to the group but are in fact ruthless individualists who view American culture and "democ-

Figure 3. Kinta, the gangster wannabe, in *Hogs and Warships* (also known as *Pigs and Battleships*).

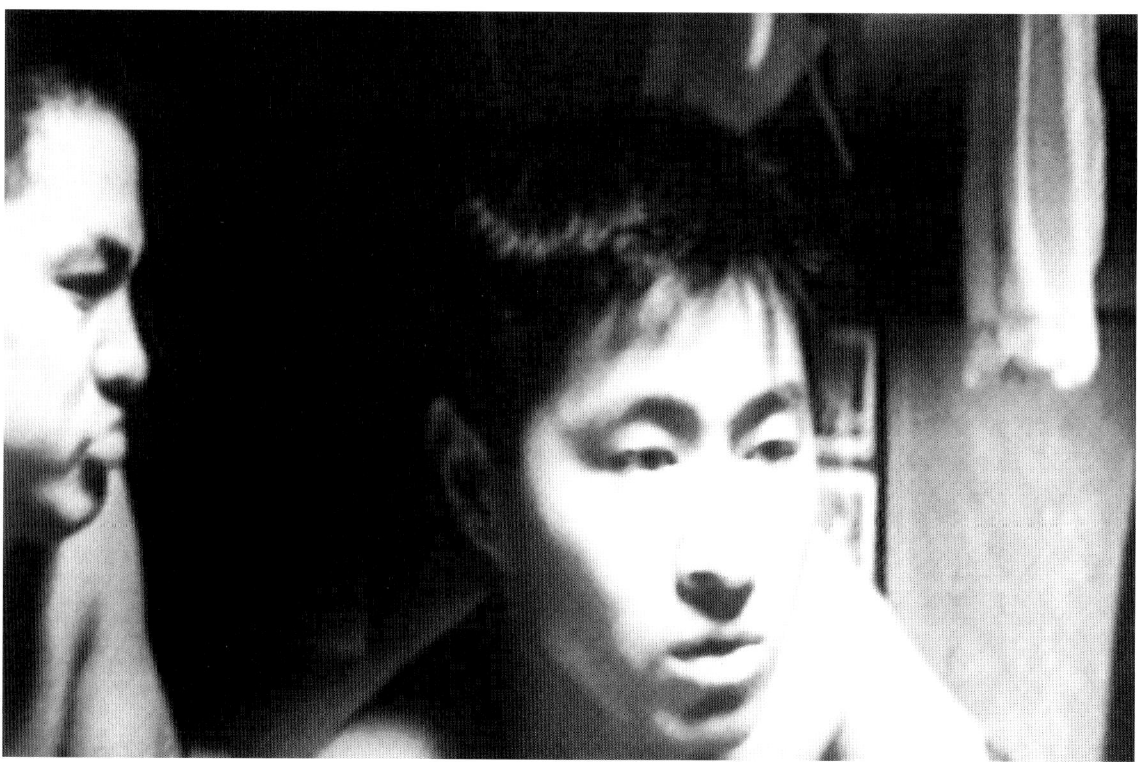

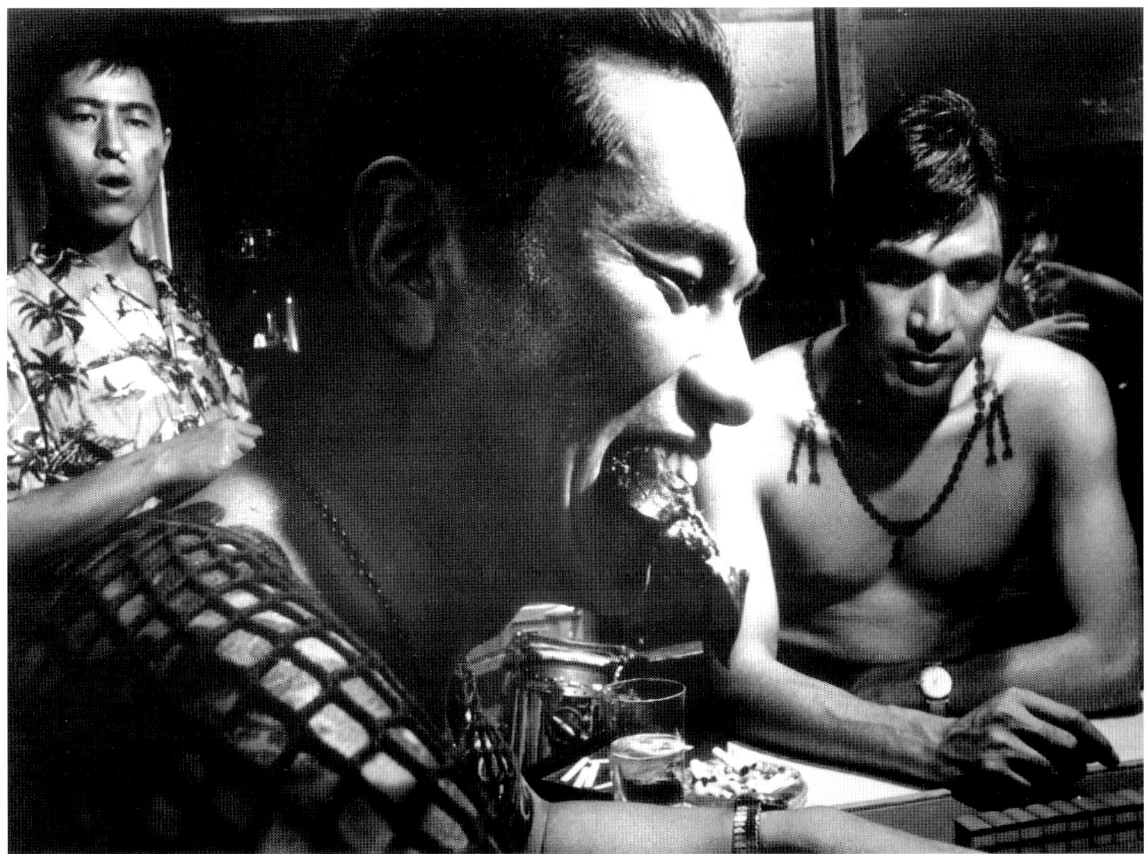

Figure 4. The gangsters in *Hogs and Warships* (*Pigs and Battleships*) espouse loyalty to the group but are in fact ruthless individualists. They view American culture and "democracy" as a source of easy money and little restraint.

racy" as a source of easy money and few restrictions (fig. 4). For them, democratization equals personal gain, at anyone else's expense. In both films, democracy is shown to be more than it first appears to average Japanese citizens, but also less than the answer to their dreams.

In a 1986 interview, Shinoda asserted that the children in his film are not necessarily unhappy about being made to erase passages in their textbooks; on the contrary, they are pleased at having less to study.[5] If that is so, then what does he mean by the scene in which the young boy Ryuta is told by his grandfather to burn the drawings of Japanese battleships he made during the war, lest they displease the American Occupation forces who will soon arrive? In this episode, the morose faces of the Japanese adults and children reveal a deep anxiety and regret about the new turn in Japan's fate. These two scenes — erasing and remembering — present different aspects of the complex Japanese response to defeat.

In actuality, there were also many paradoxes in the American stance toward "democratization" during the Occupation period.[6] For example, MacArthur advocated both a free press and labor unions, but would not tolerate either criticism of the Occupation or crippling strikes (such as the strikes at Toho film studio). Directors who belonged to leftist groups confronted unusual obstacles in filming and distributing their work. The American film censors offered a mixed view of democratization —

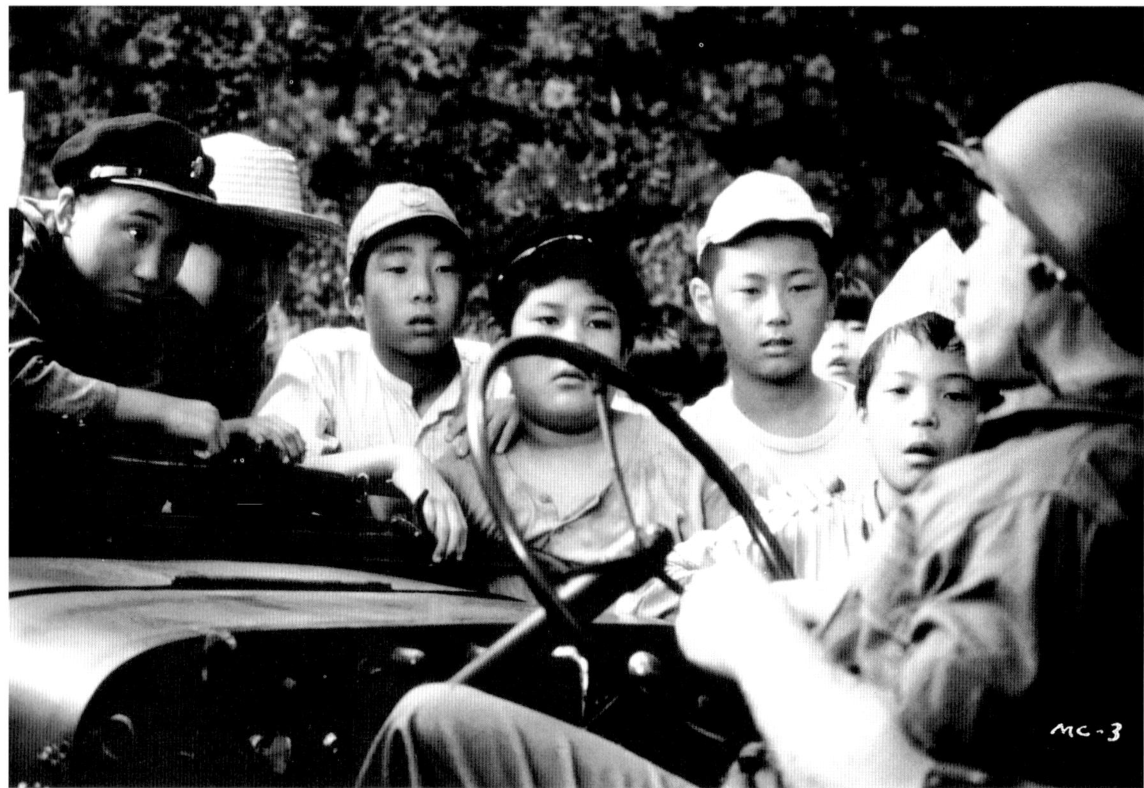

Figure 5. Both films teem with American icons, from impressive displays of tanks and planes to jazz music to the universal phrase "bye-bye." Here, in *MacArthur's Children,* young Japanese eye a GI chewing gum.

working to erase "feudal tendencies" in films (swords, displays of loyalty to a master) in favor of "democratic" norms like kissing, gunfights, and respect for women. (In *MacArthur's Children,* Shinoda presents one charming scene of a confused Japanese audience observing one of the "kissing movies" endorsed by the American censors.) And yet American movies that depicted internal problems in the United States, such as *The Grapes of Wrath* and *All the King's Men,* were not allowed in Japan during the Occupation period. Scripts for Japanese films were tampered with until they became innocuous enough. The only presentations of the atomic bomb that the censors permitted were sentimentalized ones.

Both *MacArthur's Children* and *Pigs and Battleships* are replete with Americanisms: chewing gum, comments on the supposed sexual prowess of American servicemen, jazz and swing music, displays of impressive U.S. tanks and planes, and Japanese bidding each other farewell with "bye-bye" (fig. 5). The focus is definitely more "American" than broadly "modern." While "modernization" might be seen as potentially efficacious, especially in a country sorely in need of rebuilding following the devastation of war, "Americanization" carries with it the strong suggestion of one culture being imposed on another. Both Shinoda and Imamura regard that process with some dismay.

The mixture of fear and admiration toward the foreigner that Japanese anthropologist Yoshida Teigo has found throughout Japanese history is nowhere clearer than in the subtexts of these two films recalling the Occupation.[7] Even the sardonic, swaggering tone adopted by Kinta and his gangster cohorts in *Pigs and Battleships* reveals that ultimate power is not in their hands. The battleships in the title belong to the Americans; the Japanese gangsters own the pigs that stampede through the streets. Imamura favors neither the encroaching American powers nor the often infantile gangsters. His faith resides elsewhere, in the resilient female archetype he creates.

FEMALE ARCHETYPES

At the end of *Pigs and Battleships,* a disgusted Haruko (Yoshimura Jitsuko) leaves the dead body of her former boyfriend Kinta and exits for the growing industrial area of Kawasaki to work in a factory there. As she departs, Haruko passes through a throng of giggling women waving to the next boatload of American soldiers arriving on shore. Film scholar David Desser points out that Haruko in *Pigs and Battleships* is one of the early representatives of what turns out to be a series of case studies in Imamura's work of resilient Japanese women, in touch with a deeper level of Japanese nature underneath the surface veneer of modernization.[8] This deeper level sought by Imamura often includes raw, earthy images of incest, brutal sexuality, and displays of sudden, violent emotions — a far cry from the more common image of the Japanese as reserved and as interested only in the subtle and understated.

Nine years after *Pigs and Battleships,* Imamura directed another film offering a view of the interaction between American servicemen and Japanese women during the Occupation period. *History of Postwar Japan as Told by a Bar Hostess* (Nippon sengo shi: Madamu Omboro no seikatsu, 1970) is an on-screen interview of a Madame Omboro. Interspersed with the interview are newsreel clippings of events that took place during Japan's (and her) recent history. Madame Omboro talks about her experiences during the Occupation as a member of the pariah class *(burakumin)* who became involved with American soldiers in her small bar in Yokosuka, near Tokyo. Eventually she had a child by one American sailor and later married another sailor thirteen years her junior. At the close of the film, she moves to San Diego with him, but it is implied that the resilient and intrepid Madame Omboro will strike out on her own again.

Although less polemical than *Pigs and Battleships, MacArthur's Children* also presents female characters as particularly strong and inventive. This is certainly the case with the schoolteacher Komako, who remains the moral core of the film. In addition, in the character of Hatano Mume (Sakura Shiori), the daughter of a Japanese war criminal (fig. 6), Shinoda offers a somewhat pessimistic view of the future generation:

> **In *MacArthur's Children,* I feel the greatest violence in the character of the young girl. She doesn't foresee a normal life in normal society as part of her future. She's full of many kinds of hatred for the history of the whole era, particularly, I think, for the emperor, to whom her father was so faithful.[9]**

Shinoda's use of the word "violence" in reference to Mume gives a clue to the subtlety of his depiction of the Japanese response to the Occupation. As portrayed on

Figure 6. **The end of one way of life, the beginning of another: Mume, daughter of a convicted war criminal, and the schoolboy Ryuta look to the future in *MacArthur's Children.***

screen, Mume appears introverted and troubled, but hardly violent. While Imamura places violence and emotion directly on the surface of the characters in his film, Shinoda aims to show a glimpse of their inner core.

Near the end of *MacArthur's Children,* we learn that the father, designated a class-B war criminal, has been executed. Despite the news of her father's death, Mume joins the baseball game as a means of exorcising memories and rejoining life. Here as in *Pigs and Battleships,* it is a female character who inspires faith in a true redefinition of postwar Japanese society.

STICK FIGURES

Just as Hollywood has often romanticized the "East," so do films like *MacArthur's Children* and *Pigs and Battleships* offer a rather one-dimensional view of Americans. Neither Shinoda nor Imamura dwells on the kind of fear the Americans might have felt in approaching their former enemy on Japanese territory. Rather, the Americans are presented as they might have appeared to the Japanese at that time — broad-brushed figures projecting an air of self-assurance and invulnerability.

In *MacArthur's Children,* there is one comic sequence in which anxious Japanese villagers peer from behind tall grasses at empty streets as the Americans roll into town. Thoughtless American soldiers, walking on tatami mats in their army boots or playing with the severed head of a Bunraku puppet, are reprimanded by more sensitive members of their staff, but they all still march noisily through the streets singing "Army Boogie" in unison. The Americans take their jeep for a joyride up the steps of a Shinto temple, with Japanese children racing close behind.

In scenes like these, Shinoda seems content to point out cultural differences between the exuberant Americans and the outwardly more constrained Japanese. One senses that the director's loyalties might be more complex, however, when the apparently well-meaning American soldiers are seen spraying Japanese children with large quantities of DDT: the film was made in 1984, long after DDT's dangers had become known.

In *Pigs and Battleships,* the presence of Americans in Japan is equated with corruption, greed, and a kind of moral cancer, like the cancer that one of the key gangsters believes has invaded his body. The Japanese, like the pigs — which are fed on the garbage from U.S. naval ships and then sold on the black market — are shown as ultimately dependent on the Americans and lacking in basic common sense. Even the relatively clear-headed Haruko reports having attended a party and danced the samba, and later is raped by a group of drunken American soldiers. At their worst, the Americans in these films share in the general chaos; at their best, they can construct only fragile bridges between two different ways of life.

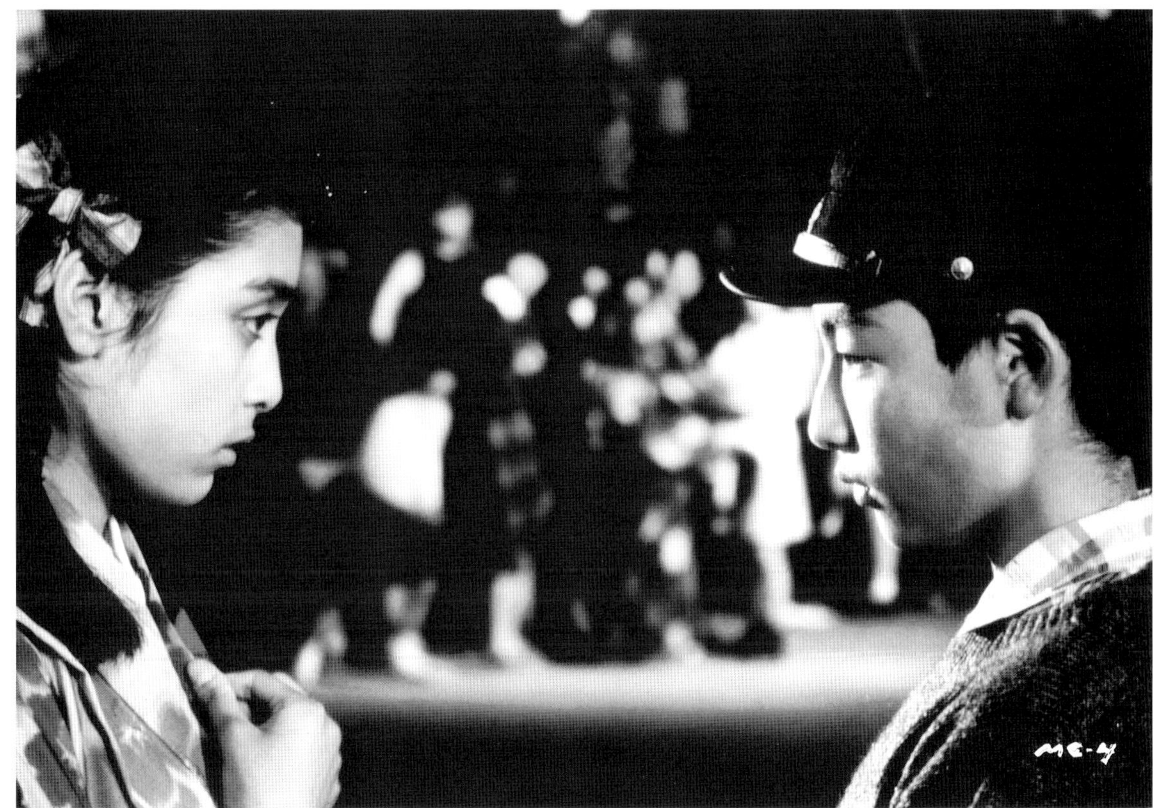

PERSONAL MEMORIES

The actual problems many Japanese city-dwellers faced were far more acute than either film implies. With transportation systems near collapse and serious food shortages, the early Occupation period was far less picturesque or exhilarating than the two films suggest. Then again, the situation was somewhat less grave in the countryside and in the smaller cities on the periphery of the island chain, where the films are set.

Shinoda has elaborated on his own feelings about defeat:

> **To be defeated in war is a very sweet experience. Winning is only transitory, while being defeated involves this problem inside ourselves for a long time. However, whether Japan became greater through this is questionable.[10]**

As film scholar Leger Grindon has pointed out, movies set in historical times are a means of "grappling with the present by writing about the past." The historical-fiction film, as distinct from the documentary, can be, at its worst, an artificial creation, shut off from reality. Yet it can also represent a serious engagement with historical issues and an attempt, through its characters and story line, "to synthesize the individual and collective causes operating in history."[11]

One has to ask what films like *MacArthur's Children* and *Pigs and Battleships* have to say not just about the Occupation era but also about the times in which they were made. While Imamura's film is filled with the forward-looking, raw energy still apparent as Japan rebuilt itself during the 1960s, Shinoda's film from the 1980s reflects a time when the Japanese could pause in their frantic race toward modernization and reflect on the rapidly receding memories of the past thirty years.

Shinoda is aware that his film is both a depiction of a past event and (to use Grindon's term) an "address to the present":

> **Now the Japanese have plenty to eat and live a full life, so maybe at last they can have the leeway to look at the images of their own defeat. I may be a member of the last generation that remembers MacArthur calling us cultural twelve-year-olds. . . . Since I was already fifteen, it pained me greatly that he put me at the twelve-year-old level. That statement may have been the first inspiration for this movie. The boys in this movie are twelve years old.**[12]

MacArthur's Children and *Pigs and Battleships* — acts of remembrance — record what was essentially a period of erasing and rewriting. Just as the grandfather in *MacArthur's Children* tells his grandson to burn his pictures of Japanese battleships, so do the Japanese as a whole turn away from earlier expressions of nationhood. It is easier, however, to burn a child's pictures than a memory. As the elementary-school teacher Komako passionately instructs her young students: "Our souls are not under occupation."

If films cannot always promise historical truth, they can at least offer an encounter with the power of memory. In characters like Komako, Haruko, Kinta, and Masao, Shinoda and Imamura have sketched out Japanese perspectives on the Occupation, and so have endowed a historic era with human proportions. ●

NOTES

I would like to thank Milestone Film and Video, East-West Film Classics, the Japan Film Library Council, and Ace Pictures for their assistance in procuring materials for this essay.

1. Other Japanese films that refer to the Occupation period include *Mr. Shosuke Ohara* (Ohara Shosuke-san, 1949) by Shimizu Hiroshi, in which a powerful landowner is forced to turn over a large part of his land to his tenant farmers, and Kumai Kei's *Japanese Archipelago* (Nihon retto, 1965), an exposé of several Occupation-era murder cases with possible connections to U.S. Army Intelligence. Neither film is available in the United States.

2. Gérard Grugeau, "Cochons et Cuirassés, le Pornographe Zegen: Shohei Imamura et la petite histoire du Japon," *24 Images: La revue Québécoise du cinéma* 38 (Summer 1988): 68.

3. Shinoda displays his concern with wartime Japan in his film *Takeshi: Childhood Days* (Shonen jidai, 1990), set in a mountain village in the final year of World War II. Like *MacArthur's Children,* it focuses on a group of children whose power struggles mirror the political struggles in the larger society. The conflict between the village bully Takeshi and the weaker (but more intelligent) city boy Shinji who is evacuated to the country during the Tokyo bombings parallels the kind of changes that will occur in postwar Japan as knowledge replaces physical strength in the rush toward modernization.

4. Kyoko Hirano, "An Interview with Masahiro Shinoda," *Cineaste* 14, no. 3 (1986): 51.

5. Ibid.

6. These kinds of paradoxes are made clear in Kyoko Hirano's pioneering study of the relationship between the Occupation and Japanese film, *Mr. Smith Goes to Tokyo: Japanese Cinema Under the American Occupation, 1945–1952* (Washington, D.C.: Smithsonian Institution Press, 1992). Hirano analyzes the contradictions implicit in Occupation policies, including the way the American cold war mentality tarnished the Occupation staff's view of democratization.

7. Yoshida Teigo, "The Stranger as God: The Place of the Outsider in Japanese Folk Religion," *Ethnology* 20, no. 2 (April 1981).

8. David Desser, *Eros Plus Massacre: An Introduction to the Japanese New Wave Cinema* (Bloomington: Indiana University Press, 1988), pp. 122–23.

9. Quoted in "Dialogue on Film: Masahiro Shinoda," *American Film* 10, no. 7 (May 1985): 13.

10. Hirano, "Interview with Shinoda," p. 51.

11. Leger Grindon, *Shadows on the Past: Studies in the Historical Fiction Film* (Philadelphia: Temple University Press, 1994), pp. 1, 6.

12. Quoted in "Dialogue on Film," *American Film,* p. 11.

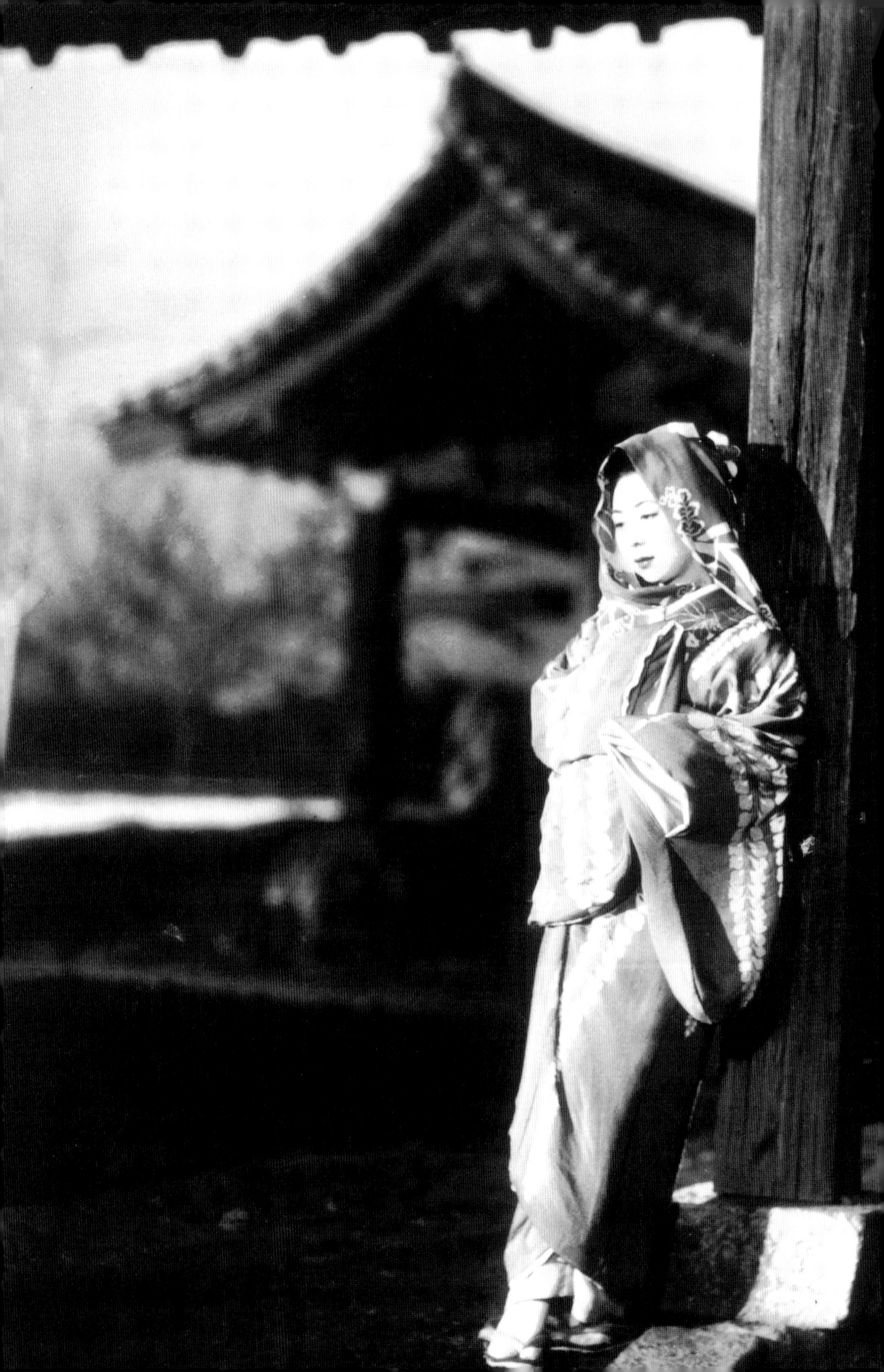

Whatever Happened to Passive Suffering? Women on Screen

KEIKO I. MCDONALD

Japanese cinema's first divas were men dressed as women. The nation's classical theater — Kabuki — had always used *onnagata,* or female impersonators, to play female parts, so that tradition, transferred to cinema, prevailed in Japanese movies made before 1920. After that time, stars could be born into either sex. Women's roles in film were played by women, some of whom became stars, although in real life Japanese women continued to be subordinate to men.

Of course, instances of female insubordination did occur. *Sisters of the Gion* (Gion no shimai, 1936), a classic by Mizoguchi Kenji (1898–1956), studies the lives of two geisha with very different attitudes about the plight of women in a male-dominated society. One is a traditionalist, accepting her fate as a servant and plaything of men. The other cannot reconcile herself to this status. In the end both are punished fairly equally, being, after all, only women. Even though the status of women provoked a great deal of thought in Japanese society before World War II, there was little action to improve it.

The real impetus toward equality came with the American Occupation and all the social and political changes it wrought before Japan regained full independence in 1952. The new constitution of 1947, for the first time, recognized Japanese women as the equals of men. Changes in the civil code gave that equality the force of law. Adultery, for example, ceased to be a specifically female crime; it became a moral issue, no longer a legal one.

These changes were preceded by an interesting example of one form of censorship taking over where another left off. During the war (as in the West), the Japanese government kept a strict watch over the Japanese film industry. Films were expected to serve the war effort in subject and approach. After the war, Occupation authorities, in turn, used film censorship as a means for recasting Japanese society in a distinctly different mold. The Civil Information and Education Section (CIE), the agency in charge of film censorship, banned thirteen themes associated with the "nationalism" of the past. Among them was any theme which "portrayed favorably the subjugation or degradation of women."[1] This new board of censors was paying cinema the backward compliment of recognizing its power to depict and influence real life, for good or for ill.

Before the war Japanese directors had offered numerous

Oharu (Tanaka Kinuyo) in *The Life of Oharu,* 1952, directed by Mizoguchi Kenji.

examples of women silently enduring their fate in a male-dominated society. One is Otoku in *The Story of the Last Chrysanthemum* (Zangiku monogatari, 1939), set in the feudal world of Kabuki. This maidservant lives and dies, entirely devoted to advancing the career of an aspiring Kabuki actor. After the war, however, Japanese audiences saw Japanese women trying out new roles on screen. Some of these roles were real and available; others were still largely untried, even purely theoretical. All ran counter to centuries of custom and tradition.

One might argue that the constraints of Occupation censorship helped focus the nation's attention on the new Japanese woman. Certainly films of this period show a lively interest in the subject. Their approaches range from blatant propaganda through subtle persuasion to outright fantasy. Some were stylistically conventional, others boldly inventive. Most partook of the nation's liberal mood in these difficult years of national reconstruction. Viewers were assumed to believe that Japanese society could and would come to terms with its new woman. During the second year of Occupation (1946), Japan's cinema industry began its recovery by producing some 160 films. Among them, eight were made with heavy CIE involvement. Two dealt with women's new roles in Japan.[2]

KINOSHITA, MIZOGUCHI, AND THE "NEW WOMAN"

Morning of the Osone Family (Osoneke no ashita, 1946) by Kinoshita Keisuke (born 1912) works from a script written by the leftist playwright Hisaita Eijiro (1898–1976). This film about two hard-pressed women in wartime learning to be assertive was voted best picture of the year by *Kinema Jumpo* (literally, "A Ten-Day Report on Cinema"), the most prestigious cinema journal in Japan.

The story takes place in the last two years of the war in the Pacific. The Osones are a prominent family suddenly brought low when their eldest son is arrested by the wartime military police and accused of being a liberal and therefore subversive. The plot advances by way of various obstacles surmounted by the widow Osone and her daughter. Their greatest trial arises out of their need to challenge the traditional response to their situation: women bereft of fathers, husbands, and sons must come under the protection of a male relation. The man in this case is a cousin, Colonel Osone Kazunori. He moves in, expecting to govern as head of the household.

All the characters in this film tend to stereotype, so Kinoshita gives us a stock military despot making life miserable for two traditionally submissive, long-suffering females. Prewar Japanese cinema was rich in domestic drama of this kind, and the outcome was predictable: the heroines would sacrifice themselves for some higher cause embodied in the male. Such films were vastly popular with female audiences well acquainted with the pleasures of a good long cry.

In Kinoshita's film, the widow Fusako and her daughter Yuko endure the bullying colonel until the end of the war. Then, after Japan's defeat, they rally and defend themselves. Even so, the film ends on a conventional note. Yuko's fiancé survives the war and marries her. Fusako, who has lost her younger son in the war, is reunited with

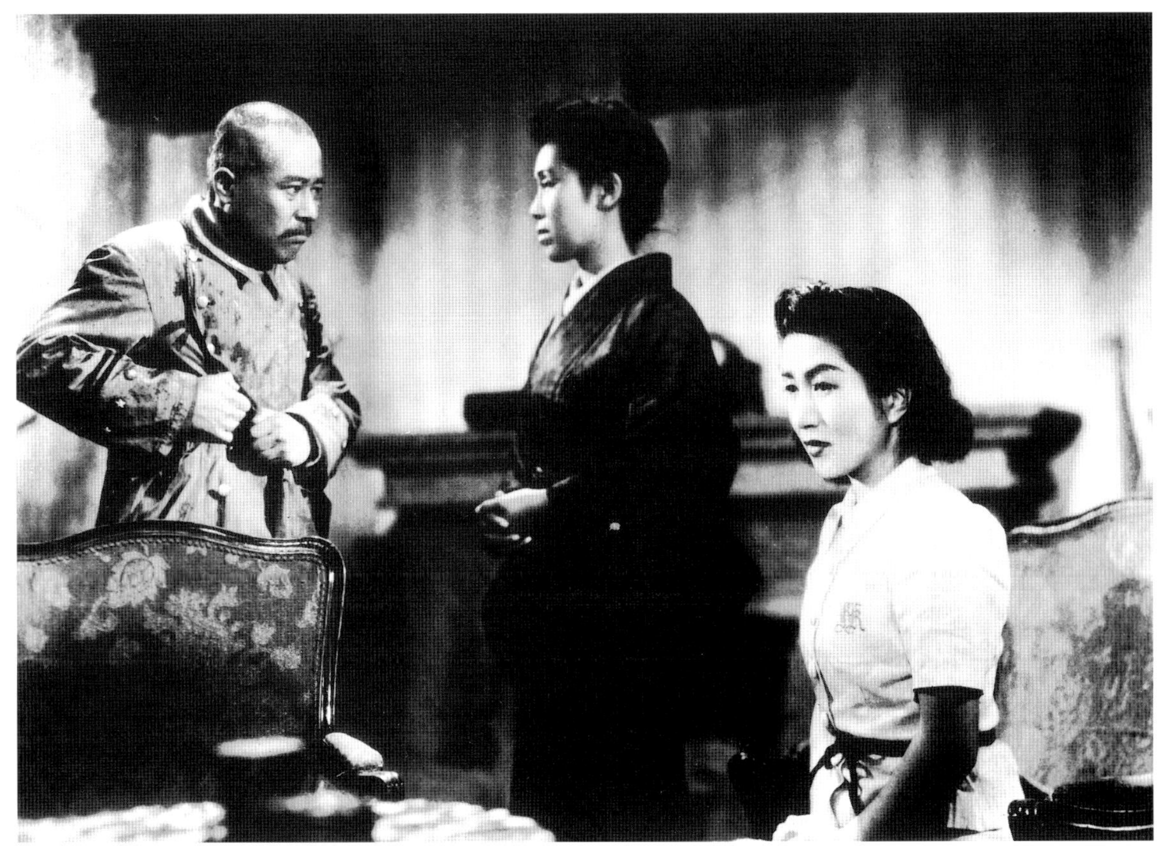

Colonel Osone Kazunori (Ozawa Eitaro), widow Fusako (Sugimura Haruko), and daughter Yuko (Miura Mitsuko) in *Morning of the Osone Family,* 1946, directed by Kinoshita Keisuke.

her elder son, released from prison by Occupation authorities.

However unwillingly, Kinoshita knew how to compromise with censorship: Colonel Osone had to be a bully and a cheat; Fusako's son had to owe his freedom to the right higher power. The film's final shot had to be upbeat and inspirational. It shows a sun rising up from the ocean — what better symbol for a nation rising from defeat.[3]

Fortunately, Kinoshita also found ways to rise above propaganda. He experimented with effects borrowed from the theater, assisted by some of the best acting talent of the day — Ozawa Eitaro (1909–1988) as the colonel and Sugimura Haruko (born 1909) as Fusako. Kinoshita's on-stage approach also owed something to postwar shortages. Elaborate sets were out of the question in 1946. Except for its opening and closing shots, this film was shot indoors. It begins with a long lateral pan showing us the outside of the Osones' Western-style house. We hear "Silent Night" being sung. A cut to the interior introduces us to the Osone family, panning to each in turn as they sing. Like the choice of music, this fluid motion of the camera speaks for the enlightened sense of freedom this liberal family enjoys. It prepares us for the shock of their son's arrest and imprisonment.

Most of the time the camera's persistent view shows characters boxed in by their surroundings. This close-in framing reinforces the viewer's sense of the oppressive atmosphere created by injustice. Making the best of his limited resources, Kinoshita presents a convincing drama of human suffering within the confines of the Osone

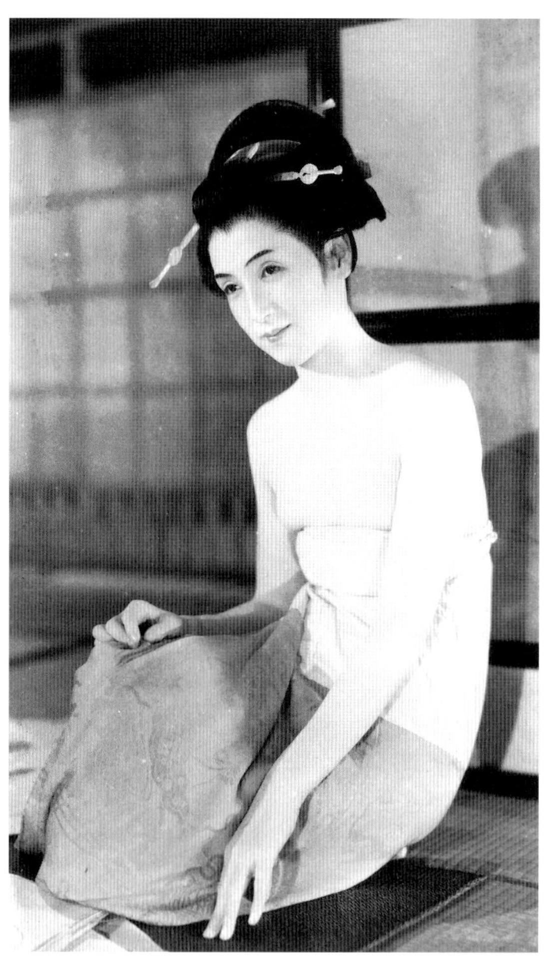

Oran, one of Utamaro's models (Kawasaki Hiroko), in *Utamaro and His Five Women,* 1946, directed by Mizoguchi Kenji.

house. The staging of people and furnishings reflects the fate the women suffer and then learn to reject.

Styles of family confrontation differ East and West, but any viewer of this film can see the change of atmosphere when, finally, Fusako stands up to the colonel and his wife. Kinoshita's camera maintains a steady view of the scene in a shot lasting more than three minutes as she enters the room and remains standing, not respectfully across from the couple but firmly and assertively between them. She returns the colonel's gifts — goods slyly taken from military stores in the confusion of Japan's surrender. The camera pans left to frame Fusako and the colonel as she denounces him at length: "You destroyed the Japanese nation and made many people suffer. Now you deserve to suffer, too!" Fusako also holds the colonel responsible for the ruin of her family, but her indictment clearly extends to the entire wartime government. She ends by telling the colonel and his wife to get out — now.

Sugimura Haruko brings a fine dramatic intensity to this scene and its wordless aftermath, when a close-up shows her leaning against the door she has closed on her enemies. In her, the viewer sees the long-suffering woman who has learned to take matters into her own hands, finally feeling free to do what she knows is right.

The second "new woman" film passed by the censors in 1946 was Mizoguchi Kenji's *Victory of Women* (Josei no shori). This work would be the first in his trilogy of "feminist" films. The other two were *The Love of Actress Sumako* (Joyu Sumako no koi, 1947) and *My Love Burns* (Waga koi wa moenu, 1949). *The Victory of Women* reverses Mizoguchi's prewar approach to the woman-centered themes that were his mainstay first and last. Before the war his heroines nobly, if tragically, sacrificed their own happiness to the demands of a male-dominated, money-oriented society. After the war they struggled for independence.

The Victory of Women begins with the release of political prisoners that was part of the Occupation's policy for democracy in Japan, and Mizoguchi's plot also illustrates one aspect of this process. The heroine Hiroko is played by Tanaka Kinuyo (1909–1977), destined to star in most of Mizoguchi's postwar films. She comes on the scene in a notably liberated role familiar in the West today — the successful female trial lawyer. Her foil is familiar, too. Her younger sister Michiko is a submissive wife

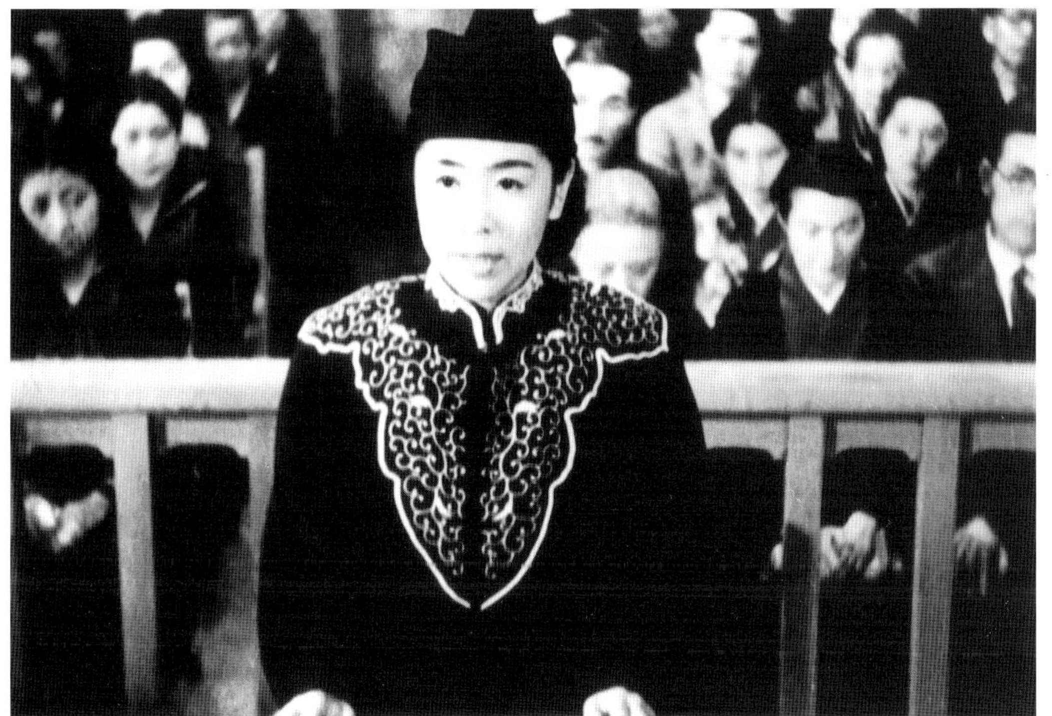

Hiroko (Tanaka Kinuyo) in ***The Victory of Women,*** **1946, directed by Mizoguchi Kenji.**

and daughter-in-law — the embodiment of traditional Japanese womanhood. Their men contrast accordingly. Hiroko's fiancé Yamaoka is a liberal journalist imprisoned during the war. He is pitted against Michiko's husband Kono, the hard-nosed state prosecutor who sent him to prison.

The opposing value systems represented by these couples have their day in court. Kono and Hiroko clash as prosecutor and defense in the case of a woman accused of infanticide. Mizoguchi, never one to overlook a melodramatic opportunity, adds to the tension by having Hiroko argue her case even as her fiancé lies dying of causes related to his long imprisonment.

Mizoguchi's trademark subtlety — especially his fluid camera work — is missing from this film. He stages a conventional courtroom climax seen in an exchange of close-ups. Hiroko, center screen, declares that her client is a victim of a military regime that deprived her of a husband and thereby of all that a woman in her place needed to survive. Style and theme join in portraying Hiroko as a paragon of strength and dignity. But this scene has an air of contrivance, of a director straining to comply with censorship demands. The effect is unmistakable, but the intent is too obvious to be convincing.

The conflict of values in the script offers Mizoguchi a chance to dramatize the more personal transformation of Hiroko's sister, who becomes aware of woman's subjugation in response to Hiroko's courtroom eloquence. But although she rejects the traditional role of dutiful wife and daughter-in-law, personal connection is missing. In the end, she talks like a mouthpiece for the liberation party line: "The most fortunate woman in the world is the one who can stand by herself. . . . I am no longer dependent on men."

Mizoguchi's next film, *Utamaro and His Five Women* (Utamaro o meguru gonin no onna, 1946), also celebrates the new official policy on women and freedom. Here, too, there are signs of censor-pleasing, but this script offers the familiar weight and feel of history, as it is set within the restrictive social framework of feudal Japan.

Utamaro and His Five Women gives that edifice a shock by showing the artist Kitagawa Utamaro (1753–1806) embroiled with five females in the throes of awakening to self and self-fulfillment. Each woman's conflict involves having to choose between the classic Japanese ethical poles of *giri* (social obligation) and *ninjo* (personal inclination). All five opt for *ninjo* in varying degrees and suffer accordingly.

Takasode, one of Utamaro's models, is a courtesan, hired to please men, yet she follows her heart and elopes with a lover. Oran, another model, refuses to be a plaything of a feudal lord and betrays her class by eloping with an artist's apprentice. Yukie, daughter of a distinguished painter, challenges patriarchal authority by leaving home to be closer to her fiancé. Oshin trades the working security of a house of prostitution for the uncertain financial future of marriage to Utamaro's servant apprentice. Okita, another model, is the primary focus of the film. She follows *ninjo* in a fight to the death with feudal oppression. Rejected by a weak and fickle lover, she stabs him and her rival, who is Takasode.

Mizoguchi is famous for shooting a scene without any cut to develop the drama in a given situation (the one-scene, one-shot method). He aims a steady camera at events taking place, letting subtle changes of focus give the viewer a sense of being an intelligent witness. For example, following the double murder, the camera views Okita from the bust up as she walks down the hallway leading to Utamaro's room. The slightly tilted camera in the same shot takes note of her disheveled hair and her obvious emotional disarray. Utamaro and Oshin and Yukie come into the hallway. The camera pans to follow them into the living room. There they all sit. Then the camera's high angle takes note of the room's partitions. This shot conveys the boxed-in, captive feeling of characters caught in the press of intense emotion. Okita says: "I'll be punished for this. But there's no choice because I did not want to deceive myself in love."

The camera holds steady but deepens its focus on Yukie and Oshin. This slight change in texture draws our attention to their shock at this defense of *ninjo*. We sense that these women have caught their first glimpse of the tragedy that can accompany passion and freedom. The camera shifts to keep Okita in frame as she stands. Then we see her in close-up — something rare in this film. The camera's long study of her face suggests that she is both resigned and victorious. She disappears from the frame, leaving us to assume that her crime of passion is an indicator of a strength of character that made her truly free to choose.

KUROSAWA AND OCCUPATION CENSORSHIP

The young Kurosawa Akira (born 1910) can be seen responding to pressures of Occupation censorship in *No Regret for Youth* (Waga seishun ni kuinashi, 1946), which offers a paradigm of the liberated woman following the dictates of her own ego and discovering self-worth through suffering. Looking back on the thirty-odd films of his career, Kurosawa had this to say: "It is only this film and *Rashomon* that focus on the woman. . . . When I made this, I firmly believed that to respect the self or ego was of primary importance for the new Japan. I still think so."[4]

The script of *No Regret for Youth* is based on two troubling episodes still fresh in the minds of Japanese audiences in 1946. In 1933 the liberal professor Takikawa Yukitoki had dared to criticize the imperialist policies of the government, which used underhanded means to deprive him of his post at Kyoto University. Then, in the so-called Sorge spy case of 1941, the same forces tried and executed one of the professor's students. The script adapts those two incidents to a plot that extends their frame of reference to include the liberating effects of Japan's defeat.

The heroine Yukie, played by Hara Setsuko (born 1920) is a beautiful, well-bred, but spoiled brat daughter of the controversial liberal Professor Yagi. Noge, one of her many male admirers, sees Yukie's spirited, enlightened, liberated notions for what they are — the posturings of a vain and selfish girl — and tells her so. Still, he loves her. Noge is a genuine liberal, willing to risk defending individual rights at a time when the government views them as the instruments of sedition. His chief rival is the conservative Itokawa, well on his way to becoming a successful government prosecutor. Yukie marries Noge, who is soon arrested and imprisoned as a communist spy. She, too, is imprisoned briefly. After her husband's death in prison, Yukie is forced to seek refuge with her in-laws in the country, and there her real transformation begins. Kurosawa gives a deft cinematic account of her change from willful city girl to suffering political exile through a newsreel style of reporting. In a dramatic montage of footage that lasts some twenty minutes, we see Yukie's suffering caught from various angles.

Yukie (Hara Setsuko) and her mother-in-law (Sugimura Haruko) in *No Regret for Youth,* 1946, directed by Kurosawa Akira.

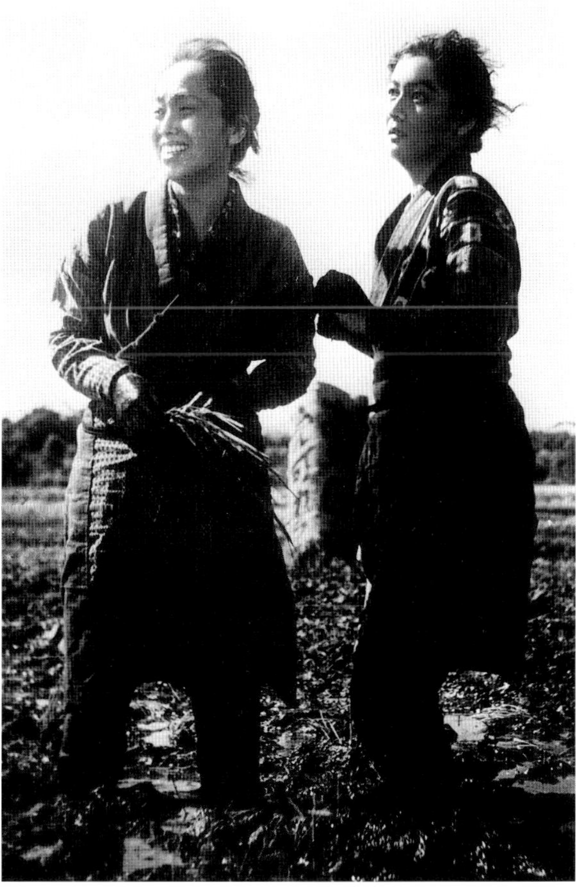

The once beautifully cared-for Kyoto belle is now a ragged farm woman, her hair and skin harried by wind and sun, her face set in bitterness from overwork and hardship. Basket on back, she moves wearily past unfriendly country people. The camera pans from one reaction to another. Children skip along, calling out "Spy! Spy!" Men look at her in disgust. Protectively, a woman hurries her child away. Two old women in close-up express hateful loathing.

A series of cross-cuts suggests that even nature disapproves of Yukie. Gathering firewood, she struggles under the weight of an enormous basket. The camera draws us into her perspective — trees looming high overhead appear to mock her weakness, to jeer at her downfall. Is she entirely cut off from human sympathy? No one is in sight. Then, as she teeters on the verge of collapse, her mother-in-law appears to shoulder the basket herself. Kurosawa pursues his theme in a montage chronicling the two women sharing the burden of hard work on the land. Close-ups repeatedly invite reflection on the difference between Yukie's smiling, self-satisfied expression in the city and this hardened, sweaty face of honest country labor.

Voice-over narration pinpoints the sources of Yukie's moral strength. She "hears" her father and husband encourage her to take the enlightened view: "No regret in my life. There is sacrifice in the struggle for freedom." The camera views the two women from afar in a series of shots observing their progress; steadily they plant and harvest despite a harsh environment. Part of their progress is human, too. Yukie's father-in-law, at first unwelcoming, softens as hard work and right thinking transform her. Her new enlightenment and self-awareness are balanced, compatible with traditional values like filial piety. We see Yukie greeting her father-in-law, kneeling to bow low on the tatami mat. What a contrast to Yukie in an earlier scene, in which the haughty, egoistic daughter of a professor orders one of her suitors to kneel in front of her! The montage of the women working together ends with a close-up showing the mother-in-law smiling at Yukie. Yukie in close-up smiles back — just as she collapses.

The film ends with a brief inspirational coda celebrating Yukie's fulfillment through dedication to postwar reconstruction and reconciliation. Back in Kyoto with her mother she says, "I found my roots in the village." She sees her life's work there. She will help bring enlightenment to the place where she found it. We see her walking along a country road. Smiling villagers in a truck stop to give her a ride. As the truck speeds away in the distance, we see a close-up of her face.

BEST PICTURE OF 1947

Kinema Jumpo gave best picture of 1947 to *The Anjo Family Ball* (Anjoke no butokai) directed by Yoshimura Kozaburo (born 1911). This was probably the year's most memorable film about women. The script owes an obvious debt to Anton Chekhov's *Cherry Orchard* (1904). Its subject was a rarity in Japanese cinema at the time: the failing fortunes of a contemporary aristocratic family. Yoshimura's boldly modern cinematic style was favorably received, as was his sensational spectacle of aristocratic females taking the lead amid dynastic decline and fall.

The once-distinguished Anjo family has seen its wealth and privileged status vanish in the ruins of Japan's defeat. The Anjo males are notably weak. The head of the family, the former Count Anjo, cannot adjust to changing times. Deprived of noble rank and title in the new egalitarian Japan, he persists in believing in the importance of lineage and social prestige. His decadent elder son, Masahiko, is a commonplace philanderer, too lazy to be anything but a playboy. The two Anjo daughters, however, are more resourceful. The elder, Akiko, a haughty divorcée, is courted by the quintes-

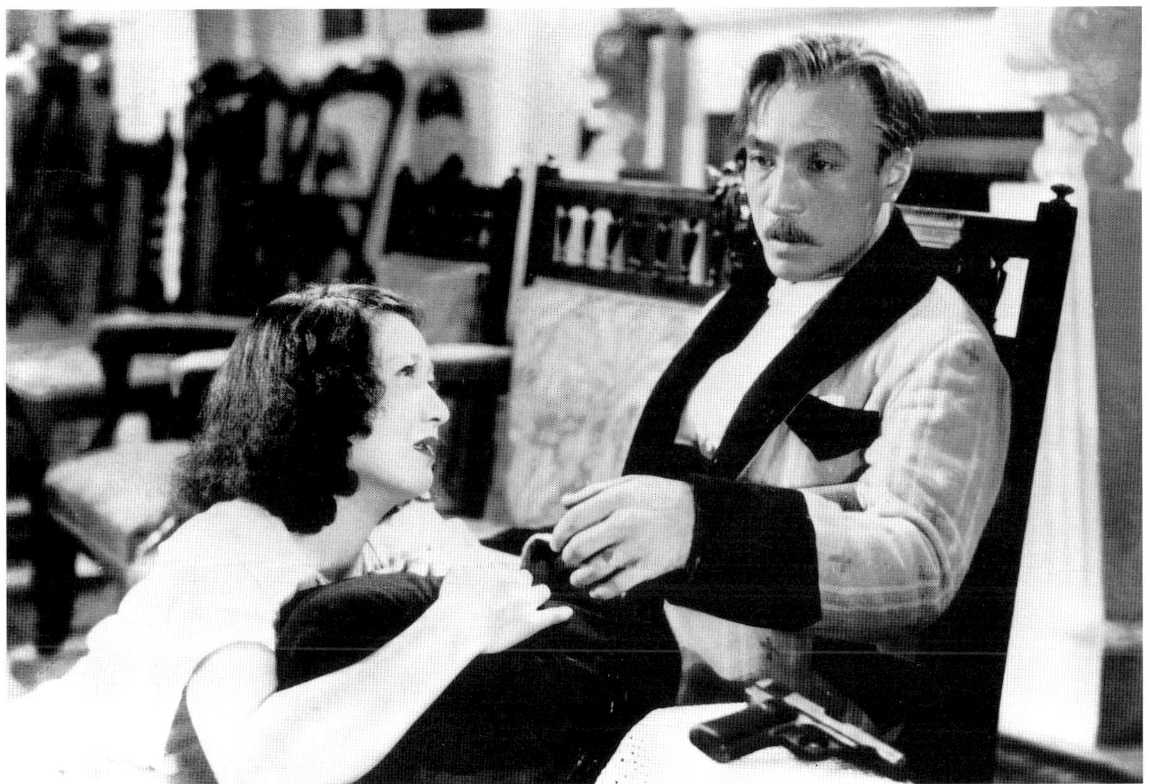

Atsuko (Hara Setsuko) and her father, the former Count Anjo (Osamu Takizawa), in *The Anjo Family Ball,* 1947, directed by Yoshimura Kozaburo.

sential newly rich vulgarian, one Toyama. This former chauffeur with a head for business has profited hugely in the get-rich-quick climate of the Occupation. Akiko pretends to despise him, but she is realistic, too. He may be beneath her, but his wealth is not.

The youngest Anjo is in every way the star of the film. She is Atsuko — played by Hara Setsuko, a hauntingly beautiful actress obviously idolized by the film's director. The character she plays gains strength from an idealized synthesis of traditional and modern values. Since her mother is dead and her father and siblings are all in their way unable to cope, Atsuko assumes the role of matriarch. She is benevolent and wise, doing all she can to help the others change with a changing world.

Atsuko is convinced that the time has come to dispense with the trappings of privilege. She puts the family mansion up for sale. To bid the old way of life a fitting farewell, she plans and presides over the ball of the film's title. She also uses this occasion to greet the new egalitarian society through a gesture that will break with old-fashioned notions of respectability once and for all: at the banquet table she announces that her father will marry his mistress.

Yoshimura is lavish with close-ups of Atsuko at the ball, taking full advantage of the statuesque beauty of Hara Setsuko, known at the time as "an eternal maiden." Atsuko is also what one might call morally lovely. Her forthright modernism is complemented by filial piety and compassion for her siblings. Yoshimura clearly considers that balance to be the driving force behind her character.

We see that balance sorely tried at the ball. Atsuko toasts Toyama as the future owner of the Anjo mansion — what better way for exhausted privilege to yield to vigorous new economic realities. Atsuko obviously thinks of matching him with her sister, but haughty Akiko rejects him in a fury. The camera follows the tipsy suitor up a flight of stairs in pursuit of Akiko. Furious and hurt, he smashes a wine glass. A series of close-ups reveals Akiko's conflicting emotions of outraged pride and amorous inclination. She is determined to get her way. A close-up of Atsuko is inserted as if to suggest that, given the compassionate concern of such a goddess, the lovers cannot fail to thrive. Akiko and Toyama are reconciled on a lonely stretch of beach where she has followed him. An extreme long shot of the two pans down to one of her high heels lying on the sand — fit symbol of pride, status, and propriety yielding after all.

The ball has ended. The guests have gone. The old count is missing. Increasing tension in the sound track music signals Atsuko's anxiety as she looks everywhere, returning to the deserted ballroom just as the sad old man prepares to shoot himself. A tilting camera records their struggle. The pistol falls to the floor. Servants rush in, but a smiling Atsuko assures them that all is well. She puts a record on to play and asks her father to dance. This is the way, she says, to start a new life. And so they dance. It seems a pity that Yoshimura mars this moment with one more touch of Anjo family soap opera. A high-angle shot of Atsuko dancing with her father turns out to be from the point-of-view of the philandering son, Masahiko, who is watching them from the top of the stairs. We see him break into sobs and rush to embrace a maidservant, his lover.

The final scene is brief but laden with significant camera gestures. As Atsuko and her father continue to dance a bolero, a pan shifts our gaze from them to a curtain lifted by the wind. We share the dancers' view of a long stretch of beach. The final shot is a last, adoring look at Atsuko's smiling face. In retrospect it seems naive, but there it is: Yoshimura, like Kurosawa, offering tribute to Japan's new woman through the beauty of a leading lady.

MIZOGUCHI AND *WOMEN OF THE NIGHT*

Mizoguchi's *Women of the Night* (Yoru no onna-tachi, 1948) studies a sadly ageless female subject. It takes its cues from Hisaita Eijiro's script *Festival of Women* (Josei matsuri), which treats prostitution as the epitome of the social and economic diseases undermining the health of postwar Japan. Mizoguchi's approach is starkly candid and darkly pessimistic. All three of his "women of the night" are victims of war, respectable women forced into prostitution to survive. Fusako is a war widow. Her younger sister Natsuko is a single woman repatriated from China. Kumiko, a sister of Fusako's husband, has lost both father and brother and so must live without the protection of a male. In traditional Japan, a woman without a husband or male relative could be forced to consent to a degrading relationship. *Women of the Night* demonstrates how easily such dependent arrangements lead directly to prostitution. The film's three case histories pose questions of individual choice as each woman seeks to rise above the condition of being used and disposed of like a commodity.

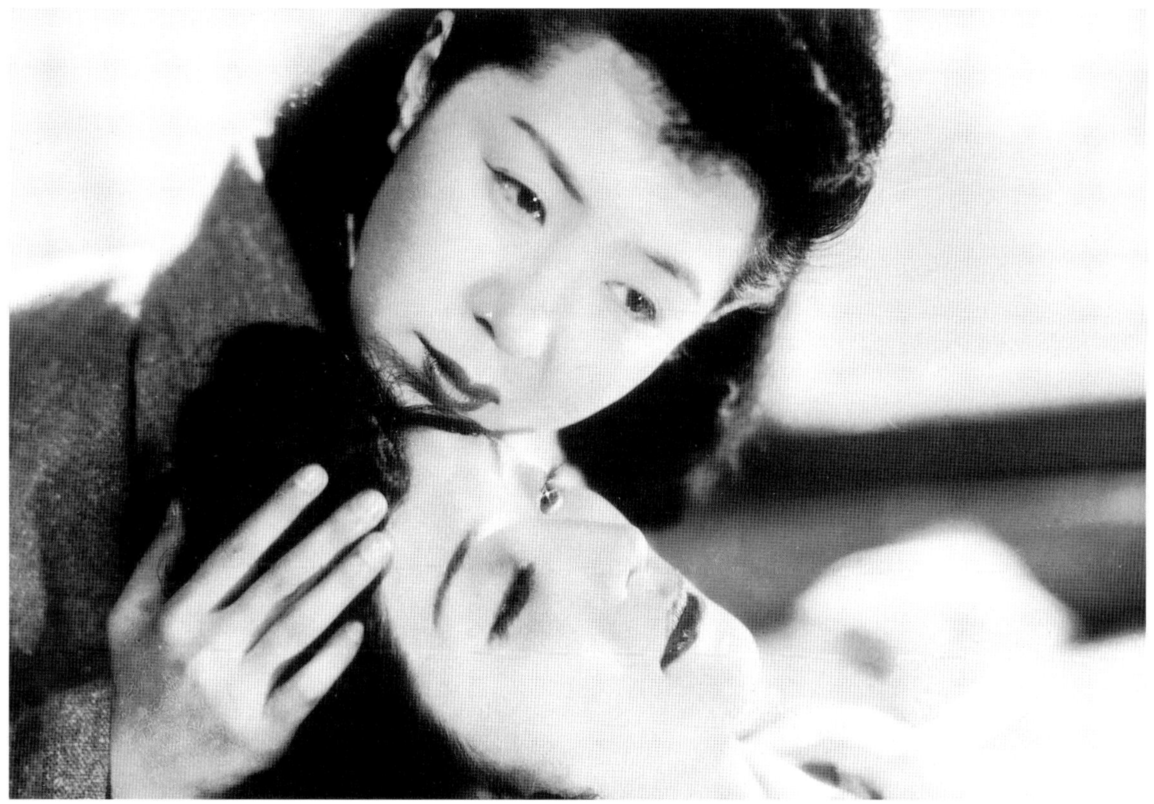

Fusako (Tanaka Kinuyo) and her sister Natsuko (Takasugi Sanae) in *Women of the Night,* 1948, directed by Mizoguchi Kenji.

Fusako's story illustrates the point and gives the film its overarching structure. Mizoguchi follows her degradation step by step. First she is a dutiful wife, mother, and daughter-in-law. With her husband away at war, and lacking earning power, she survives by pawning various family possessions. Her husband is killed. Then their only child dies. Those deaths break the ties between her and her in-laws. She has no male relation to look to for help, and so she does what any woman in her place must do: find male protection wherever she can. A black marketeer, Kuriyama, hires her. It follows that she becomes his mistress. She has no rights, no security. She is helpless to intervene when Kuriyama preys on her sister Natsuko, who contracts a venereal disease from him and carries his possibly infected child.

The horrors multiply. Fusako comes to reject conventional social norms and decides that selling herself is the only way to free herself. While she experiences the degradation of prostitution, she maintains her capacity for independent thought. Having suffered and despaired of her life, she regains her sense of self-worth by trying to help others regain theirs. She lectures other prostitutes on the evils of their trade. She helps them all she can, but actual rescue seems out of the question. This film suggests that women as oppressed as these cannot hope for the comforts of salvation; they can only hope to endure. The ancient rule still holds: once a fallen woman, always a fallen woman.

Mizoguchi explores this dark supposition in a final sequence laden with symbolism. It takes place at night, in dismal weather, in the graveyard of a bombed-out church. The camera takes advantage of a crater to focus an unusual shot upward at

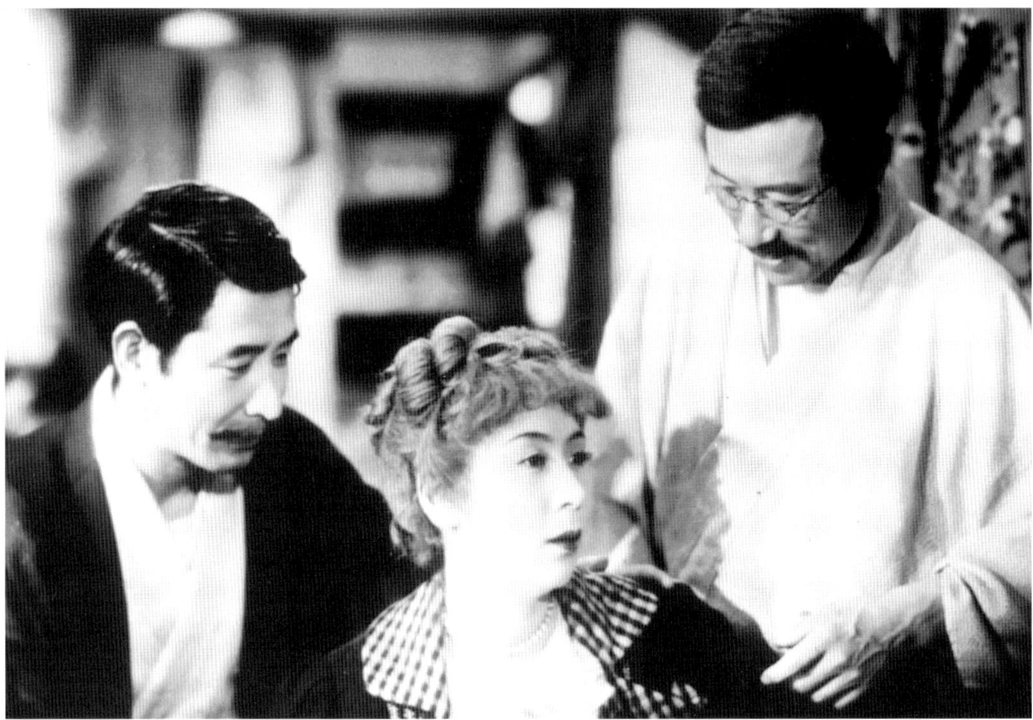

Hogetsu (Yamamura So), Sumako (Tanaka Kinuyo), and Hogetsu's teacher, Shoyo (Tono Eijiro), in *The Love of Actress Sumako,* 1947, directed by Mizoguchi Kenji.

some prostitutes who might just as well be gathering for a witches' Sabbath.

Fusako appears. The camera tracks up to follow her as she goes to the aid of Kumiko, who is being threatened as an unwelcome newcomer by this band of prostitutes. A sudden high-angle shot shows Fusako pushing Kumiko to the ground. She reproaches her former sister-in-law for having sunk so low. Torn with emotion, Fusako is shown rising above her own desperate plight to speak for all women. She urges those present to escape prostitution while there is time. A close-up of her thickly made-up face suggests a certain noble, if tragic, sincerity in her cry: "One unfortunate woman like me is more than enough." But she and Kumiko are driven off. They take refuge in a ruined church, in view of a fresco depicting the Madonna and child. The symbolism is overdone, yet the film ends in a way that seems appropriate to its subject. The camera's distant look takes note of darkness swallowing up Madonna, child, and these two doomed women huddled in ruins.

Women of the Night was followed by two films that also showed Mizoguchi responding to postwar interest in woman's freedom to define herself. The first was *The Love of Actress Sumako*, set in the late nineteenth century (Meiji period). Sumako is a woman in search of a self she can call her own. She does not find it in either of her two marriages, and she leaves her second husband to become an actress. She has, in effect, traded respectability for emancipation, like Henrik Ibsen's Nora — one of Sumako's starring roles. Sumako falls in love with Shimamura Hogetsu, an actor and innovator willing to give her an equal share in a cause that seizes her imagination — the new drama movement. Together they will reinvigorate Japanese theater by introducing audiences to the style of realism associated with Western playwrights like Ibsen and Maurice Maeterlinck. The film ends, however, on a tragic note — Hogetsu's premature death and the suicide of Sumako, who finds her professional commitment meaningless without him.

Mizoguchi ended his trilogy on women with a more complex and troubling look back at feminism's roots in nineteenth-century radical politics. *My Love Burns* is set in the 1880s, a time of social ferment and experiment led by the Movement for Freedom and People's Rights (Jiyu minken undo). The script owes a good deal to the autobiography of a leading feminist of the day, Kageyama Eiko.

We see Eiko first as an idealistic rural teenager attending a lecture by a visiting feminist. Her father and brothers strongly disapprove of this new interest. Eiko's first painful experience of social injustice comes when the family maid Chiyo is sold to a factory. Eiko is shocked by her family's casual indifference to the girl's welfare. The factory is, in effect, a sentence of hard labor in the worst conditions.

Eiko moves to Tokyo to live with her fiancé Hayase, a member of the newly formed Liberal Party. When she discovers that he is not a liberal, but a government spy on the organization, Eiko leaves him to work on the party newspaper. She goes on lecture tours with a party leader, Omoi. They marry and continue to work for women's rights.

Eiko's investigation of working conditions for women takes her to the factory where Chiyo was sold. A docu-dramatic sequence shows Eiko peering in through a lattice to see women being treated like animals, beaten by brutal overseers, and

Itagaki Taisuke, the leader of the Movement for Freedom and People's Rights (Senda Koreya), Omoi (Sugai Ichiro), and Eiko (Tanaka Kinuyo) in *My Love Burns,* 1949, directed by Mizoguchi Kenji.

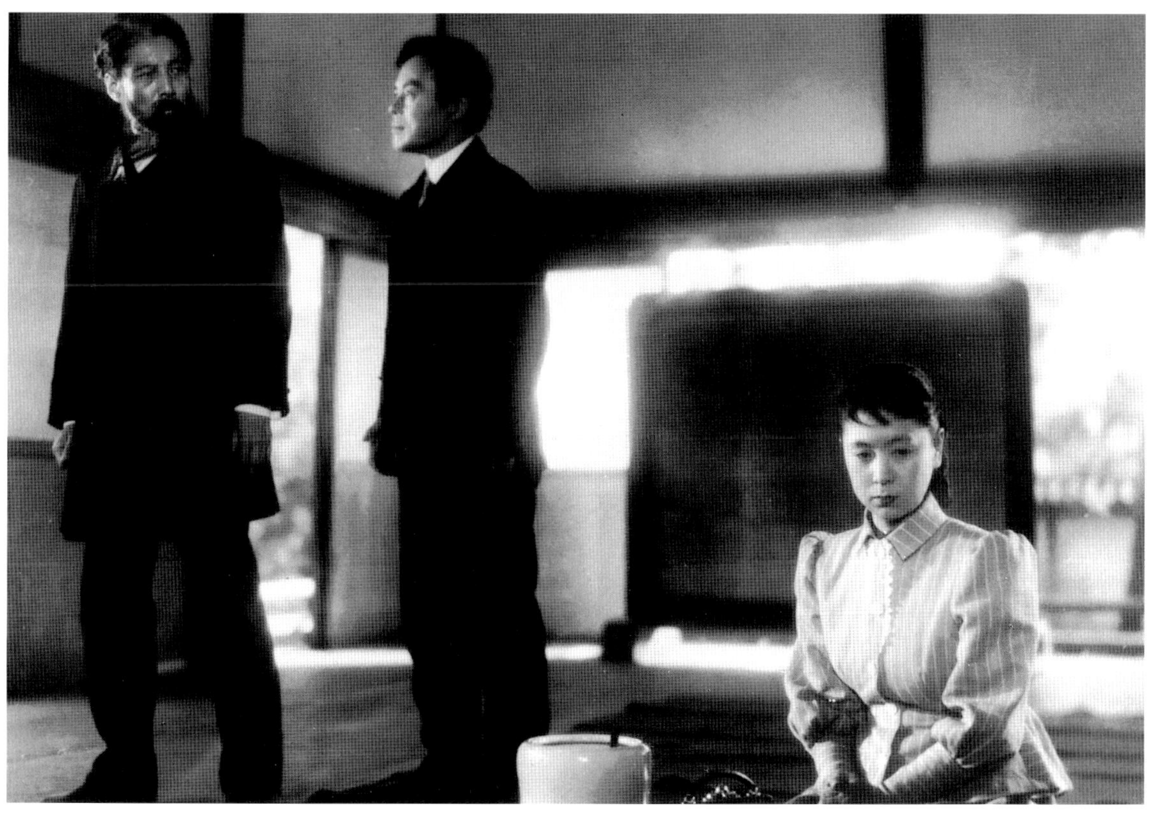

handed over to sadistic pimps. The sequence ends with Chiyo setting the factory on fire. Eiko and Omoi take Chiyo into their home, an act of kindness that leads to another incidence of male duplicity. Omoi, outspoken advocate of women's rights, cannot resist taking advantage of Chiyo. This time Eiko leaves husband and party, too. She returns to the country and founds a school where girls can learn to expect to have rights.

This highly charged film ends on a quiet, sentimental note whose point is obvious. Eiko is returning to the country on a train. Chiyo enters the carriage; both have left Omoi. A parting shot shows the two women sharing a shawl. This ending celebrates the bonding of two women in a context of enlarged personal freedom. But it leaves the viewer wondering: Will Chiyo, a former factory slave and prostitute, be accepted by the rural community? Will Eiko be accepted — she who has left a highly successful husband to accomplish something all her own, on her own? As in *Women of the Night,* Mizoguchi's portrayal of women's struggles offers no comfortable answers.

Significantly, it was *Women of the Night* rather than Mizoguchi's propagandistic feminist trilogy that played a role in effecting social changes in the status of women. Along with *The Gate of Flesh* (Nikutai no mon, 1948) directed by Makino Masahiro (born 1908), it made the Japanese keenly aware of the horror of prostitution. As a result, the Antiprostitution Law (Baishun boshi-ho; literally, "Prostitution Preventive Law") was debated a number of times in the Diet until it finally passed in 1956.

NEW CONFIDENCE

From 1947 on, those in charge of Occupation policy soon found themselves faced with a number of crises created by their very success. At first, Occupation authorities had encouraged the unionization of workers as a positive deterrent to prewar nationalism. The formation of the All-Japan Employee Union Association (known as Zen'ei) in September 1946 was one such effort. However, some newly democratized Japanese adopted forms of liberalism so extreme that government sought new controls. In 1947, Occupation General Headquarters stepped in to halt a general strike. Three strikes at the Toho Studio put serious obstacles in the way of film production from 1946 to 1948. Occupation authorities also intervened to end the third studio crisis — a 120-day strike. The founding of the People's Republic of China in 1949 had given American anticommunist sentiments a new source of anxiety quickly passed on to those in charge of Japanese affairs.

The Film Ethics Regulation Control Committee, or Eirin, was set up in this atmosphere of political turmoil in June 1949. Its stated purpose was to allow the Japanese to censor themselves, but Eirin's work was in fact closely supervised until the end of the Occupation. The American military wanted to make sure that Eirin would enforce the ban on films that glorified either nationalism or the authoritarian class society of Japan's feudal period.[5] Eirin complied with regulations modeled after the U.S. Production Code of Ethics, which saw to it that films depicted what were considered

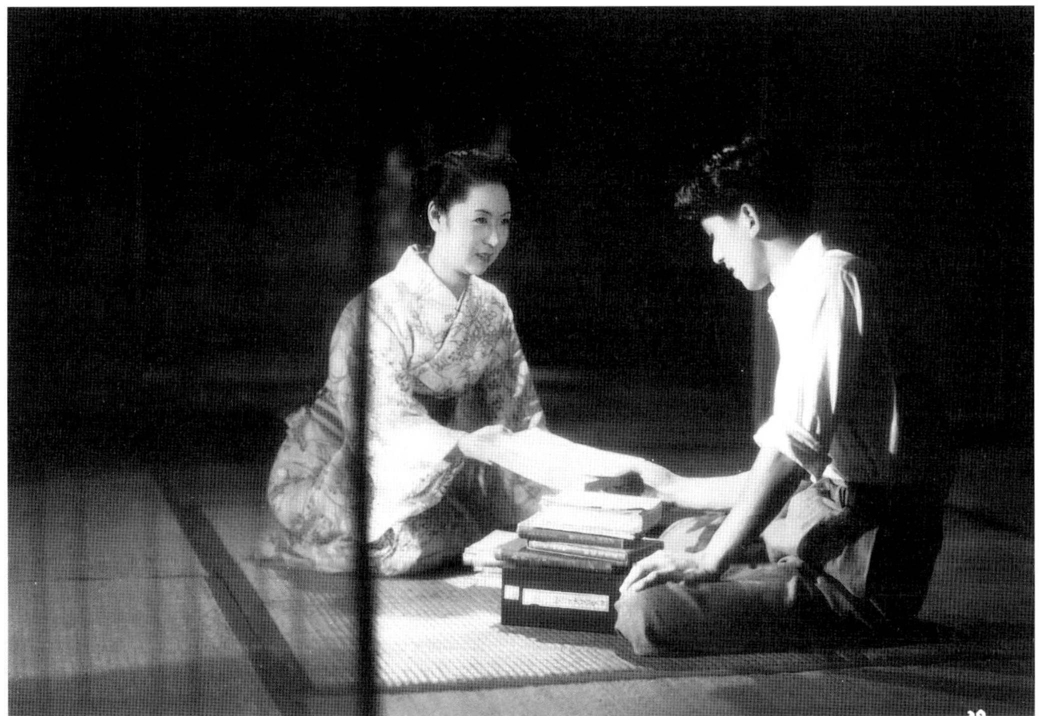

Michiko (Tanaka Kinuyo) and Tsutomu (Katayama Akihiko) in *Lady Musashino,* 1951, directed by Mizoguchi Kenji.

"proper families and decent life-styles."[6] Yet Eirin was extremely sensitive to the subject of labor unions, reflecting increasing U.S. fear of communist infiltration.

The San Francisco Peace Treaty of May 1951 paved the way for Japan's return to full independence in April 1952. By that time Japanese filmmakers were noticeably more at ease with issues relating to women. Two films stand out as representative of this new confidence. Mizoguchi's *Lady Musashino* (Musashino fujin, 1951) adapts a best-selling novel by Ooka Shohei (1908–1988), a rising star in postwar Japanese literature. The subject is adultery. Now that it was no longer a crime, Ooka used it to weigh ethical decisions freely made by upper-class women in the newly democratized Japan.

The traditional moral standard for women is represented by Michiko, who believes that a wife must be chaste. She is not proof against temptation. In fact, she is secretly deeply in love with her cousin Tsutomu, a repatriate from Burma. The new woman is represented by Tomiko, who is married to a man named Ono but thinks nothing of carrying on with her friend Michiko's husband, Akiyama. To her, such affairs are an element of more stimulating modern life. But Tomiko is also an old-fashioned opportunist. When Akiyama offers to leave his wife, Tomiko agrees to marry him — so long as he gains possession of his wife's property.

Mizoguchi's attention to life-styles makes *Lady Musashino* a film of manners as well as morals. The camera's candid eye takes in details that speak for widely differing values. Michiko invariably appears in kimono, most often properly seated on a tatami mat, surrounded by walls of honest wood in her traditional Japanese house. She is the lady of the title, a woman we never see venture away from the Musashino Plain with all its associations of unspoiled nature and time-honored ways.

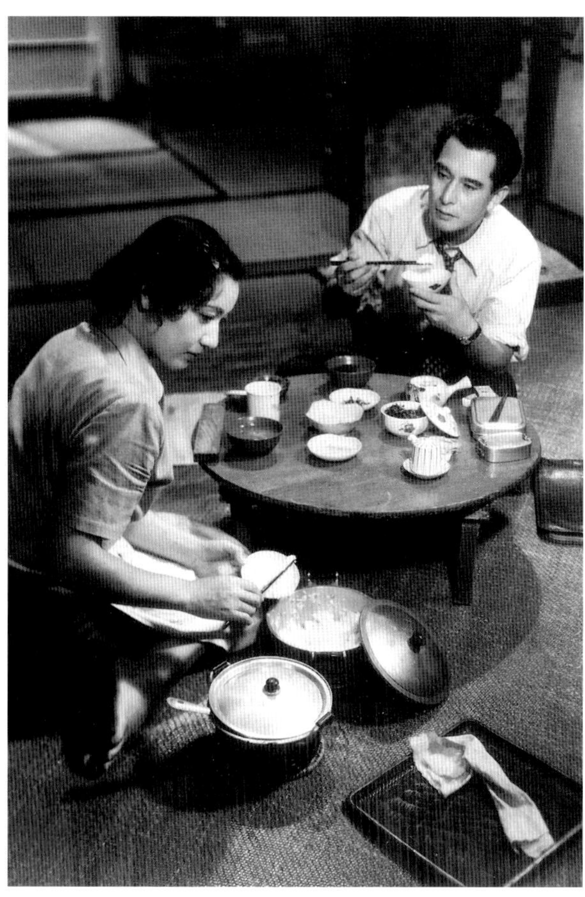

Michiyo (Hara Setsuko) and her husband, Hatsunosuke (Uehara Ken) in *Repast,* 1951, directed by Naruse Mikio.

Tomiko lives in a Western-style house set in a sprawling lawn. She moves freely in tight, low-cut dresses and is no stranger to the wicked city. We see her dancing tipsily with various men in a bar in Tokyo. Her assignations with Akiyama are also in Tokyo, where she meets Tsutomu, too.

Two such obvious extremes might strike today's viewer as overtly schematic. But in the Japan of 1951, Mizoguchi is addressing a tension experienced every day by those in his audience. Tsutomu, the character who bridges these extremes, is in some respects an idealist drawn to traditional standards of behavior. But while he transforms his deep love for Michiko into a purified devotion, he also succumbs to Tomiko's wiles.

Lady Musashino is a story of innocence betrayed — by husband, by friend, and by platonic lover. Viewers today would expect betrayal to lead to a violent death. But in Mizoguchi's melodrama emotions are the killers. And so it is Michiko who dies, killed by a disease indistinguishable from goodness. It follows that her dying works a charm on all who have betrayed her. They crowd around her bed, each transfixed with a redeeming guilt and remorse. Her husband blames himself for her death. Tomiko clings to her, weeping and begging forgiveness.

Mizoguchi's camera studies these emotions without the contemporary cynicism that stands in the way of appreciation today. Michiko is his favorite kind of heroine: the nobly forgiving, self-sacrificing woman whose destiny is to put men in touch with redemption. The camera lingers in close-up as Michiko proclaims that she must die so Tsutomu can live happily. He rises to the occasion, denouncing the materialism of the others and declaring that he will refuse all rights to the inheritance Michiko proposes to leave him.

Repast (Meshi, 1951) by Naruse Mikio (1905–1969) offers a more realistic view of domestic disarray at a time of national moral uncertainty. The script is based on a novel whose serial publication was cut short by the sudden death of the author, Hayashi Fumiko (1903–1951). Her story studies the values governing the behavior of a harried housewife trying to decide how much independence she is entitled to. The romance has gone out of Michiyo's marriage to Hatsunosuke. The daily effort to make ends meet has worn them down.

Enter Satoko, Hatsunosuke's niece. She comes from Tokyo to visit her uncle and aunt in Osaka. Satoko is young, fun-loving, and flirtatious. Michiyo finds her too shockingly modern. They clash over issues of propriety and respectability, especially in connection with men. That strain adds to Michiyo's growing unhappiness with her marriage. She becomes jealous of her niece, and she thinks her husband is spoiling the girl whom he evidently finds attractive.

When Satoko leaves Osaka, Michiyo goes too. She moves in with a married younger sister in Tokyo. Just as the novel expands on the theme of husband and wife living apart, the author's sudden death leaves it unfinished, with no clue about its outcome. Naruse, free to craft his own conclusion, creates a happy ending that celebrates the value of marriage even as new freedoms are working against it. He makes especially good use of locale and atmosphere in downtown Tokyo where, finally, Michiyo and Hatsunosuke end their separation in a touching drama of love revived.

Michiyo has, in fact, already written a letter to Hatsunosuke, telling him that she thinks their separation might as well be permanent. Now suddenly she learns that Hatsunosuke is coming to visit. She panics and leaves the house, only to run into him in the street. From afar the camera registers the ensuing chase. She hurries on ahead, but he catches up with her. Just as he does, a parade comes down the street, a joyful procession following a portable shrine. They two are trapped in the crowd and carried along by the festive music. A cut shows them taking refuge in a cheap restaurant. Hatsunosuke says in an offhand way that he has been offered a better position but has put off accepting it until he can talk with Michiyo. He adds that he knows how hard it has been for her to keep house on a small budget. Her face plainly shows that his concern has taken her by surprise. Their eyes meet. We have not seen this intimacy between them before. In a close-up, she smiles as she offers her husband the rest of her beer. He obviously savors it.

Satoko (Shimazaki Yukiko) and Michiyo's husband, Hatsunosuke (Uehara Ken), in *Repast,* 1951, directed by Naruse Mikio.

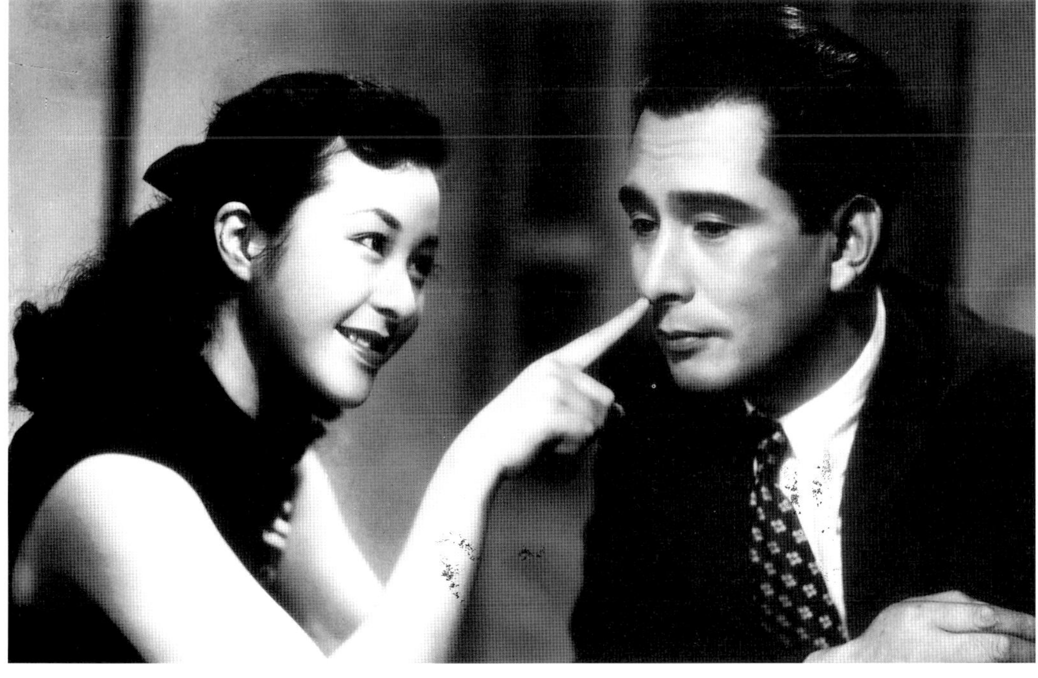

On the train back to Osaka, Hatsunosuke falls asleep beside his wife. She looks at him contentedly, tearing her letter into small pieces. Her voice-over soliloquy puts Naruse's obvious intentions into words. She has decided that a married woman's best chance of happiness lies with marriage itself — with doing all she can to help her husband in his struggle to build a life for his family in a difficult world. Naruse is not suggesting, however, that Michiyo's life will be easy. His final shot shows the couple in the downtown alley where they live. One housewife does her washing in a tub in front of her door. Others crowd round a huckster selling vegetables, all hoping for a bargain.

Mizoguchi's *Life of Oharu* (Saikaku ichidai onna, 1952), winner of a Silver Lion Award at the Venice Film Festival, is a fitting close to this brief survey of Japanese films on women during a traumatic period. Released just ten days before the end of the Occupation, it pays tribute to Mizoguchi's pre-Occupation ideal woman — the one who sacrifices for her man. But Oharu, though victimized by man's avarice and license, is far from a passive sufferer. She does forgive all, but she also does more than dissolve in all-forgiving tears. She takes action, becoming a pilgrim aspiring for enlightenment and praying for the souls of her male oppressors.

The Life of Oharu testifies to the long road Japanese filmmakers had traveled in seven years, from compromise in the face of censorship, through reconciliation with the social changes wrought by the Occupation, to an independence in the portrayal of women. But did Japanese women make the new roles they saw on the screen their own? Since the end of the Occupation many filmmakers have continued to probe this question. Notable among them is Itami Juzo (born 1933), whose heroines are often strongly independent, goal-oriented professionals. Ryoko in *A Taxing Woman* (Marusa no onna, 1988), for example, is a divorcée, a single parent, and a government official who overcomes great obstacles to climb the bureaucratic ladder. The means to her success are her own intellectual alertness and motivation, not the art of pleasing that doomed so many Mizoguchi prewar heroines. Yet it took thirty years for reality to catch up with this film image of the new Japanese woman. ●

NOTES

I would like to thank Moriwaki Kiyotaka of the Kyoto Museum of Culture for his extraordinary kindness in preparation for this article. I also thank the Kawakita Memorial Film Institute for providing me stills for reprint.

1. Kyoko Hirano, *Mr. Smith Goes to Tokyo: Japanese Cinema Under the American Occupation, 1945–1952* (Washington, D.C.: Smithsonian Institution Press, 1992), p. 44.

2. Shimizu Akira, *Senso to eiga* (War and films) (Tokyo: Shakai Shisosha, 1994), pp. 178–89.

3. Hirano, *Mr. Smith Goes to Tokyo*, p. 152.

4. Quoted in Iwasaki Akira, Hagi Masahiro, et al. *Film Directors of the World: Kurosawa Akira,* vol. 3 (Tokyo: Kinema Jumpo, 1970), p. 116. For the most cogent study of this film, consult Sato Tadao, *Kurosawa Akira no Sekai* (The World of Akira Kurosawa) (Tokyo: Sanichi Shobo, 1969), pp. 92–109.

5. Sato Tadao, *Nihon Eigashi, 1941–1959* (The history of Japanese cinema, 1941–1959), vol. 2, (Tokyo: Iwanami, 1995), p. 230.

6. Hirano, *Mr. Smith Goes to Tokyo,* p. 98.

Don't Sell Salt Illegally: Posters in Occupied Japan

JAMES HOWARD FRASER

In the eerie, quiet weeks following war's end in August 1945, Japan's poster designers and printers showed surprising resilience. Emergency and survival notices had to be printed and distributed, as did food and health announcements, all in the face of shortages so severe that even locating sheets of paper large enough for posters required scouting.

Theaters recovered quickly, and movie production hardly paused — ten feature films were released between October and December 1945[1] — so entertainment posters were also needed. Many editions were small, however, and the paper was of such poor quality that often only the ink used in the lithographic process held it together. Conversely, some posters were printed on paper thicker than usual, and so are today well preserved.

By the beginning of 1946 the domestic press, rebuilt with the aid of Occupation authorities, was supplying newsstands with a wide variety of pulp magazines, sewing monthlies, children's and young people's periodicals, photo news magazines, and even design and art journals. It seems the country needed color in that bleak time of disease, hunger, and black marketeering. Making the most of the color and economies of the poster as a means of mass communication was a predictable development.

By the end of the Occupation period the infusion of capital from the United States in the form of procurement contracts for troops now engaged in the Korean War was having a profound effect on Japan's economic recovery. As consumer goods and services became increasingly available, advertising boomed and poster design, in particular, flourished. Entertainment, tourism, and politics also increased opportunities for older designers who had survived the war as well as young designers who were graduating from design schools just in time to experience this first flush of postwar expansion.[2] ●

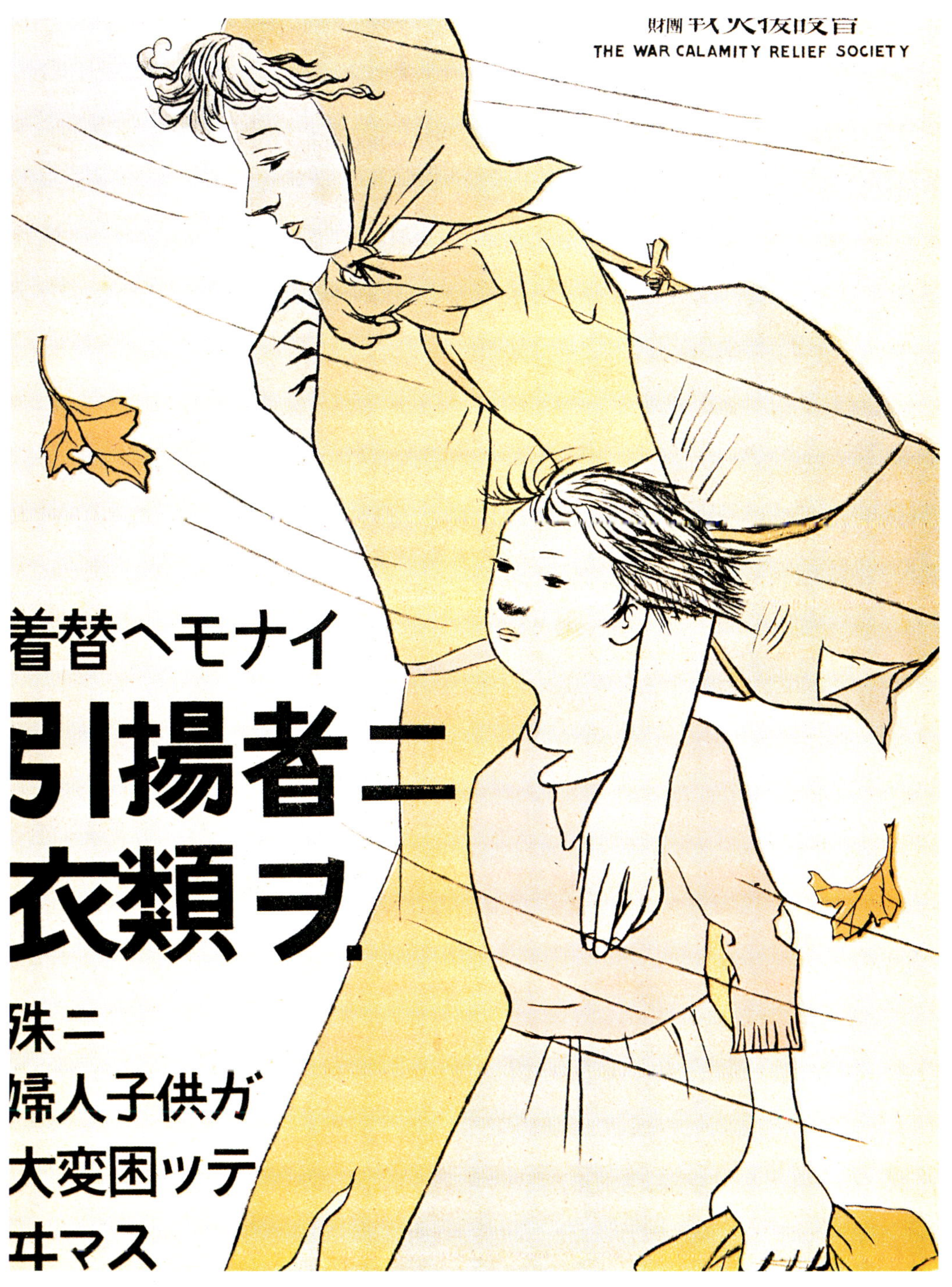

Yamana Ayao, "Donate Clothes for the Returning Refugees, Especially for Women and Children," fall 1945. Offset print, 72.5 x 72.5 cm. Shiseido

At war's end, Yamana Ayao (1897–1980), long famous as a designer for Shiseido cosmetics, turned his talents to noncommercial purposes. This somber poster for the War Calamity Relief Society called attention to the needs of Japanese refugees, particularly women and children, returning from China.

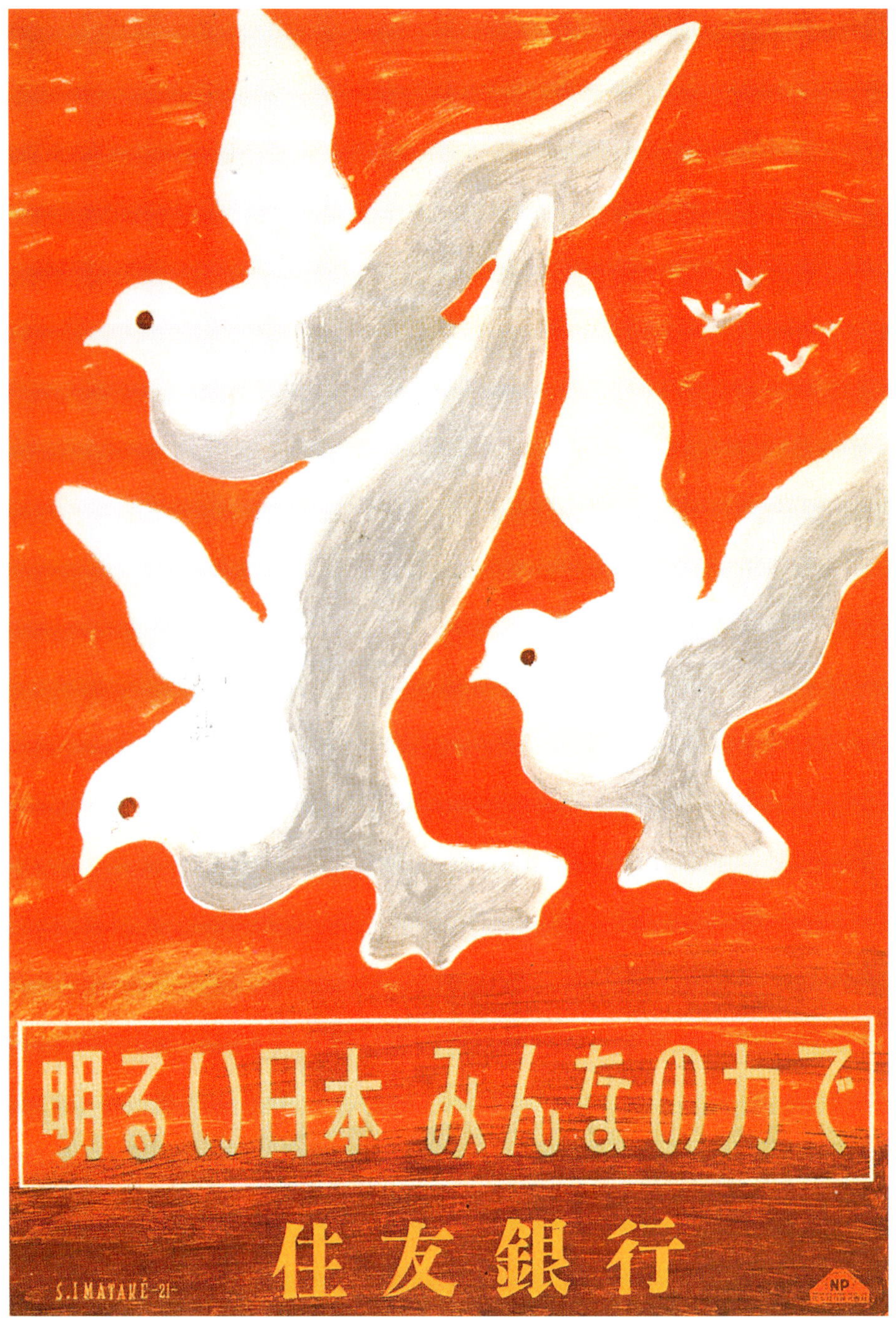

Imatake Shichiro, "Let's All Make a Bright Future for Japan: Sumitomo Bank," fall 1945. Offset print, 67 x 48 cm.

Some posters appearing in the first months after the war combined commercial advertising and public service announcements. In this poster, designed by Imatake Shichiro (born 1905) for the Sumitomo Bank, the poignant image of peace doves speaks to an issue clearly prominent on survivors' minds — peace. Imatake was a leader of the modernist movement in graphic design as well as being a noted painter.

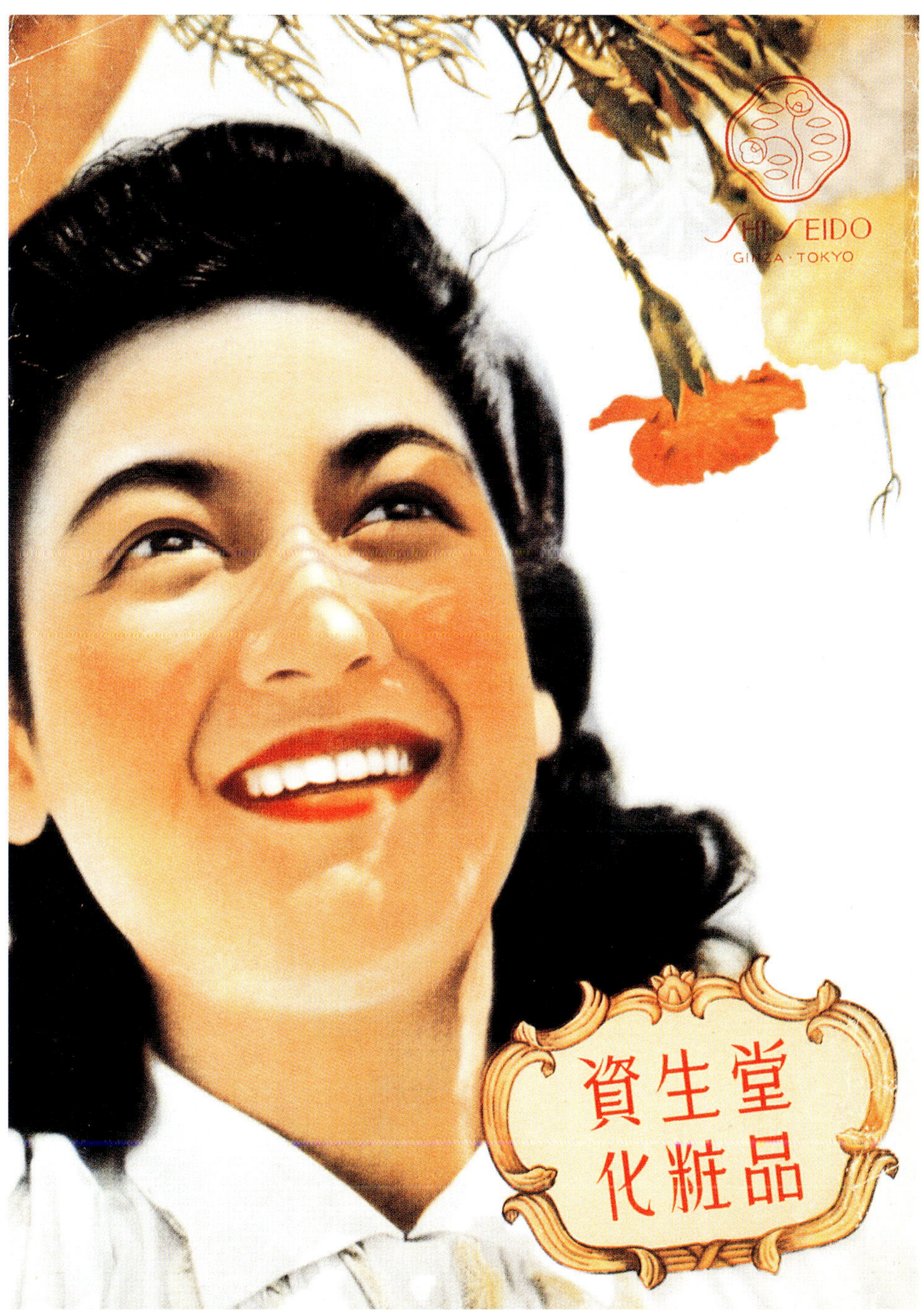

Omi Tadashi, "Shiseido Cosmetics," 1946. Offset print, 72.5 x 52 cm. Shiseido

By 1946, posters were employing hopeful images and brighter colors to take viewers' minds off scarcities and the ordeals of queuing for basic necessities. Shiseido began advertising again, and this poster by Omi Tadashi (died 1959) was intended to provide a psychological lift as well as sell beauty products. Note that his perfect-skin model sports Western dress and hairstyle.

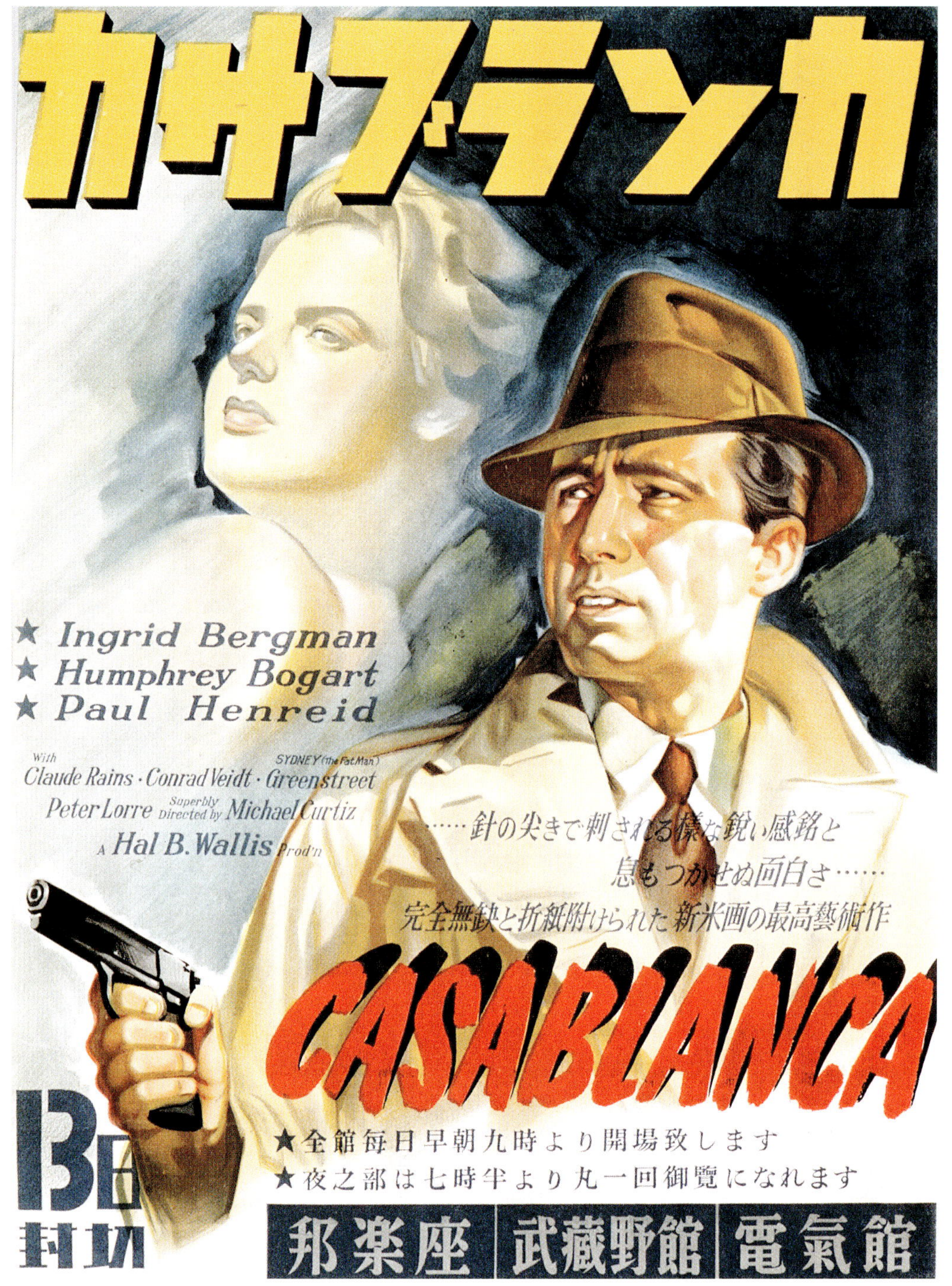

Designer unknown, *Casablanca,* 1946. Offset print, 52 x 37.9 cm. Musashino Art University, Museum and Library

Originally released in 1942, this film starring Humphrey Bogart and Ingrid Bergman was distributed in Japan in the immediate postwar years. Wartime movies from the United States and France were circulated throughout Japan during the Occupation, and posters announcing them were often modified in both text and image.

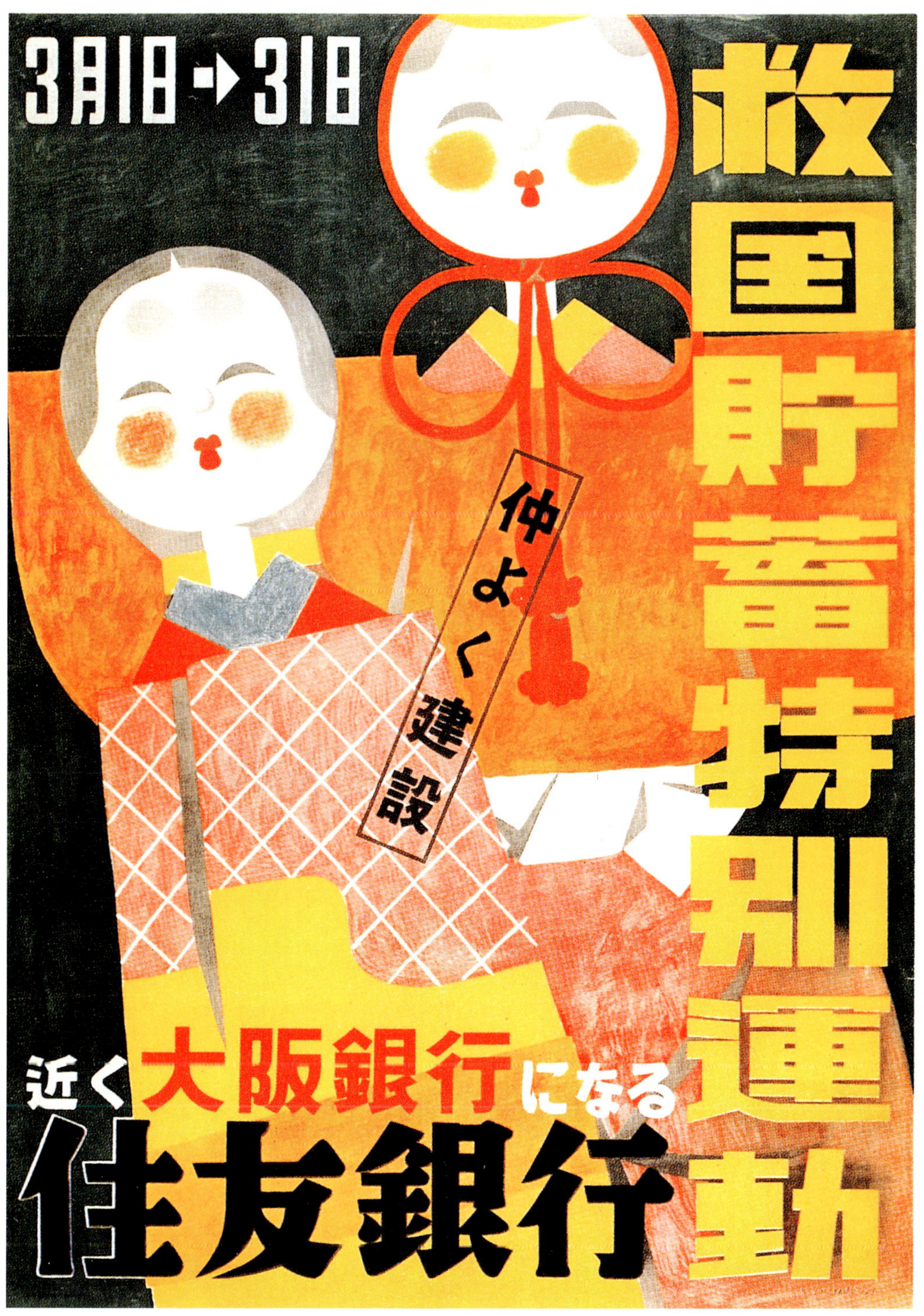

Imatake Shichiro, "March 1st to the 31st: National Bond Campaign for Reconstruction. The Sumitomo Bank Is Being Renamed the Osaka Bank," 1946. Offset print, 70 x 52 cm.

A year after his first postwar poster, the Sumitomo Bank again commissioned Imatake. Here his stylized, folk-motif design promotes a reconstruction bond campaign while simultaneously announcing the renaming of the bank.

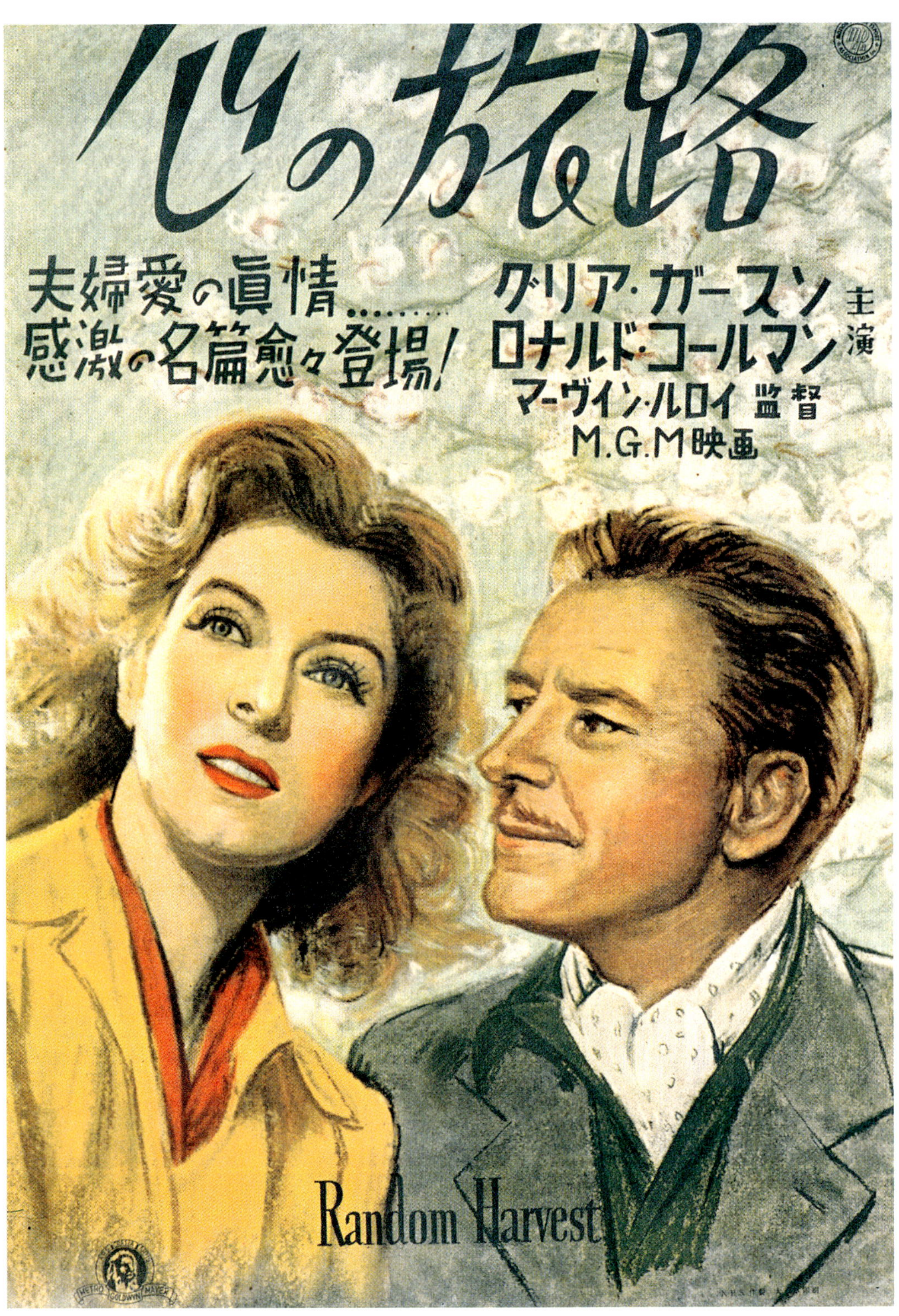

Terashima Ryuichi, *Random Harvest,* 1947. Offset print, 51.7 x 36.3 cm. Musashino Art University, Museum and Library

Originally released in 1942 and starring Ronald Coleman, Greer Garson, and Susan Peters, *Random Harvest* is here promoted in a design by Terashima Ryuichi (born 1918).

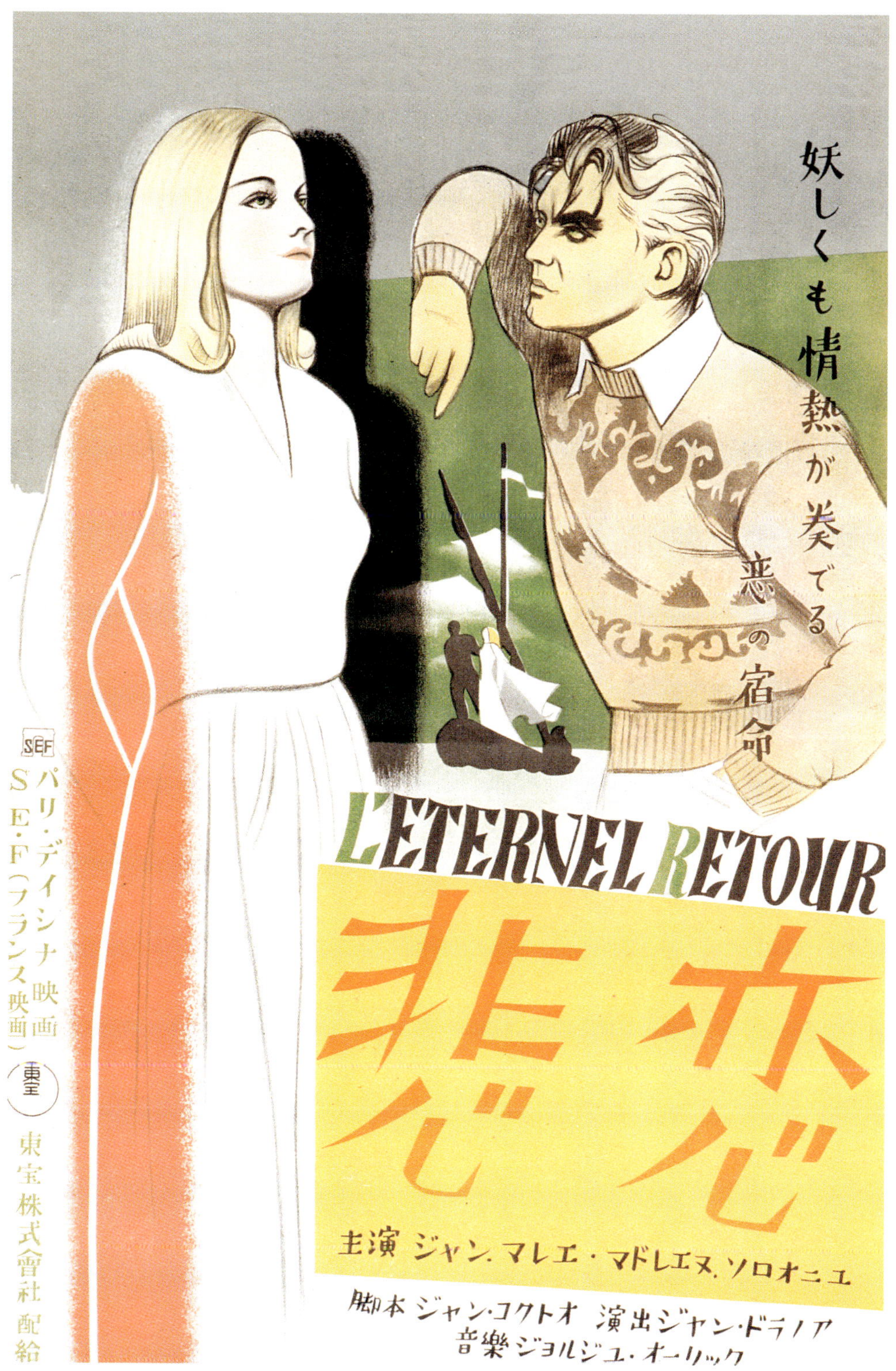

Oshima Tadashi, *Eternal Return,* 1948.
Offset print, 50.6 x 36.1 cm. Musashino Art University, Museum and Library

Eternal Return, starring Jean Marais and Madeleine Sologne, was first released in France in 1943. This design is by Oshima Tadashi (dates unknown).

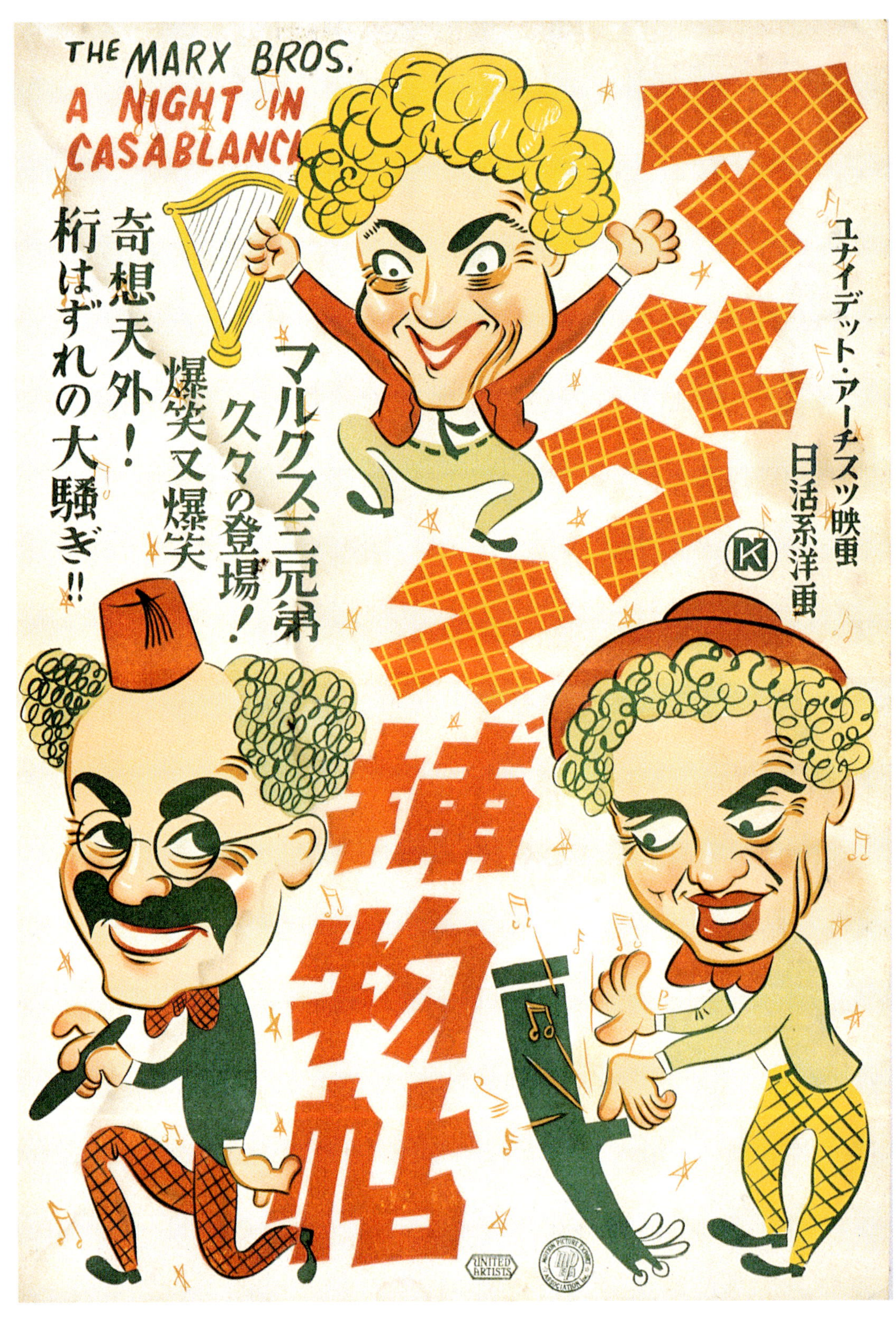

Designer unknown, *A Night in Casablanca,* 1948. Offset print, 55 x 36 cm. Musashino Art University, Museum and Library

This film, originally released in 1946, starred the Marx Brothers.

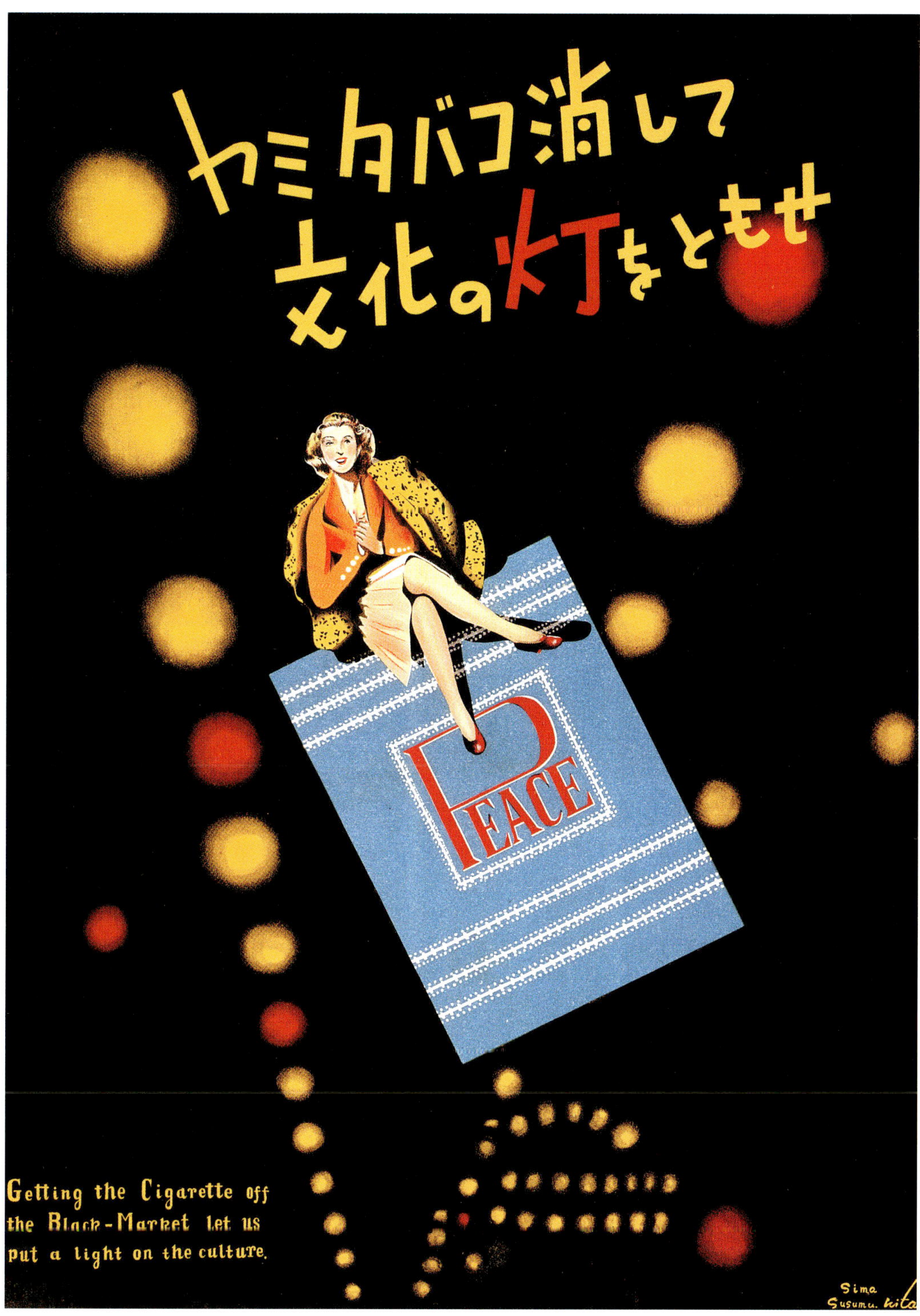

Designer unknown, "Peace Cigarettes," 1950. Offset print, 52.2 x 37.8 cm. Tobacco and Salt Museum, Tokyo

This Nihon Senbai Kosha (a government agency) poster advertising "Peace Cigarettes" carries its wishful request in both Japanese and English in what was surely a vain attempt at controlling this ubiquitous black market currency.

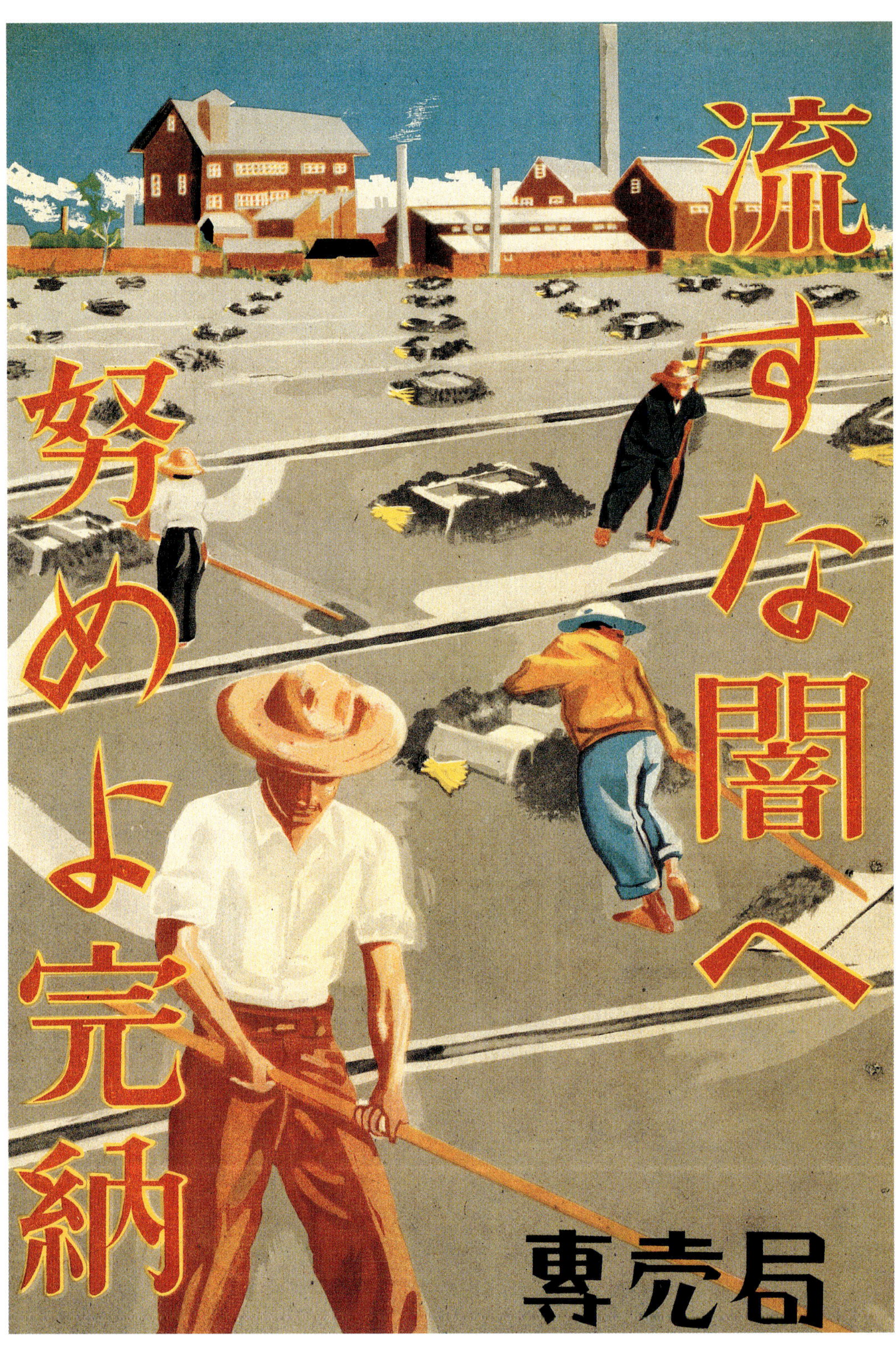

Above: **Designer unknown, "Don't Sell Salt Illegally. Make an Effort to Deliver All Your Production to the Government," 1949.** Offset print, 52.3 x 36.6 cm. Tobacco and Salt Museum, Tokyo

Right: **Tani Masuzo, "Don't Sell Salt Illegally. The World Is Monitoring Imported Salt," 1950.** Offset print, 52.9 X 38 cm. Tobacco and Salt Museum, Tokyo

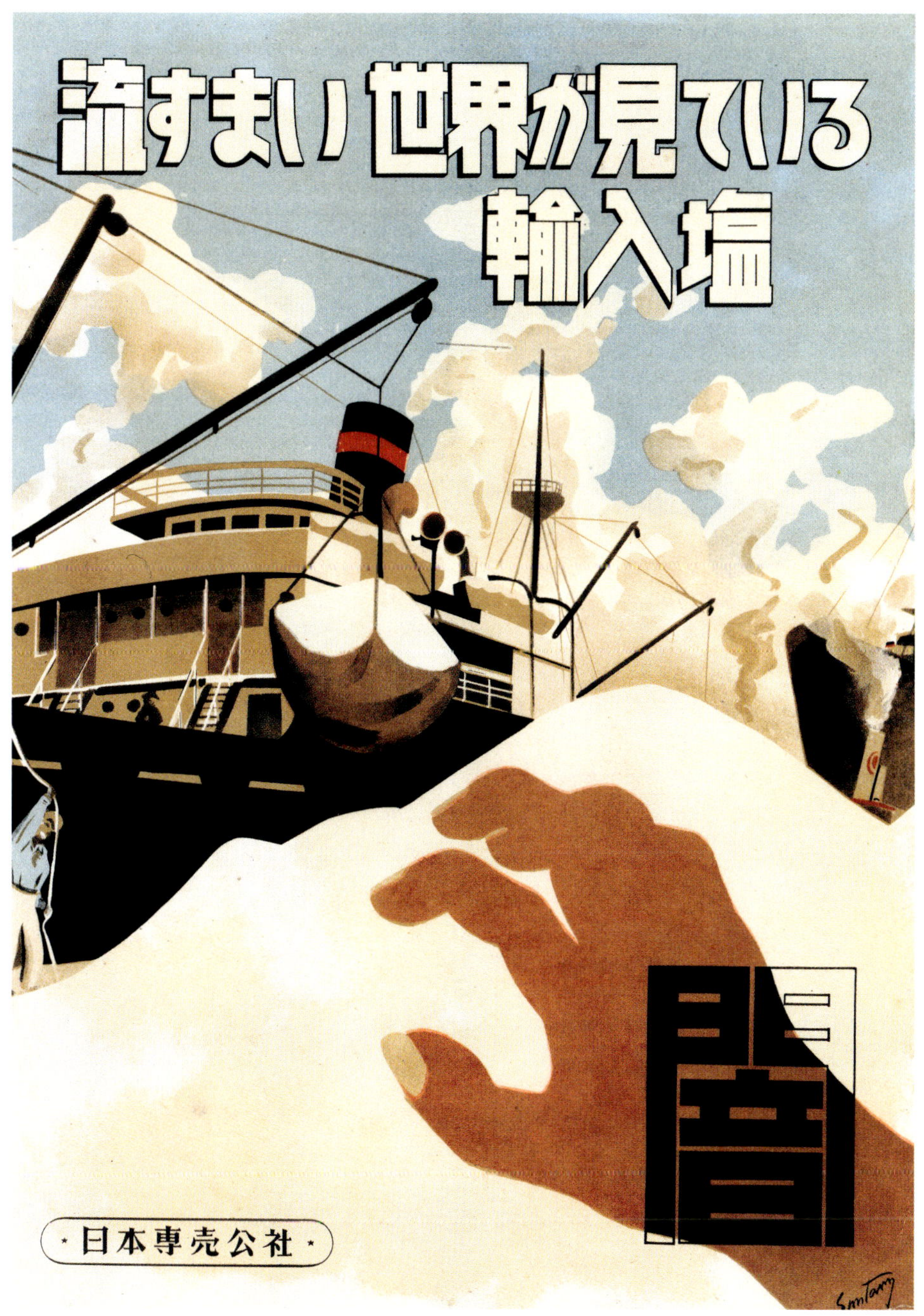

Following the death in 1947 of a Tokyo district court judge from malnutrition owing to his refusal to eat any foods that had been purchased on the black market,[3] the government launched a campaign against illegal trading. Tobacco and salt, which had been government monopolies since 1898 and 1905 respectively, were frequent black market commodities, and the government agency responsible for them, the Senbaikyoku (from 1949 to 1985 established as Nihon Senbai Kosha) produced a number of posters, including these two, urging citizens to comply with government regulations. The second is by Tani Masuzo (born 1913), although, like many posters of the era, both lack the designer's signature and monogram.

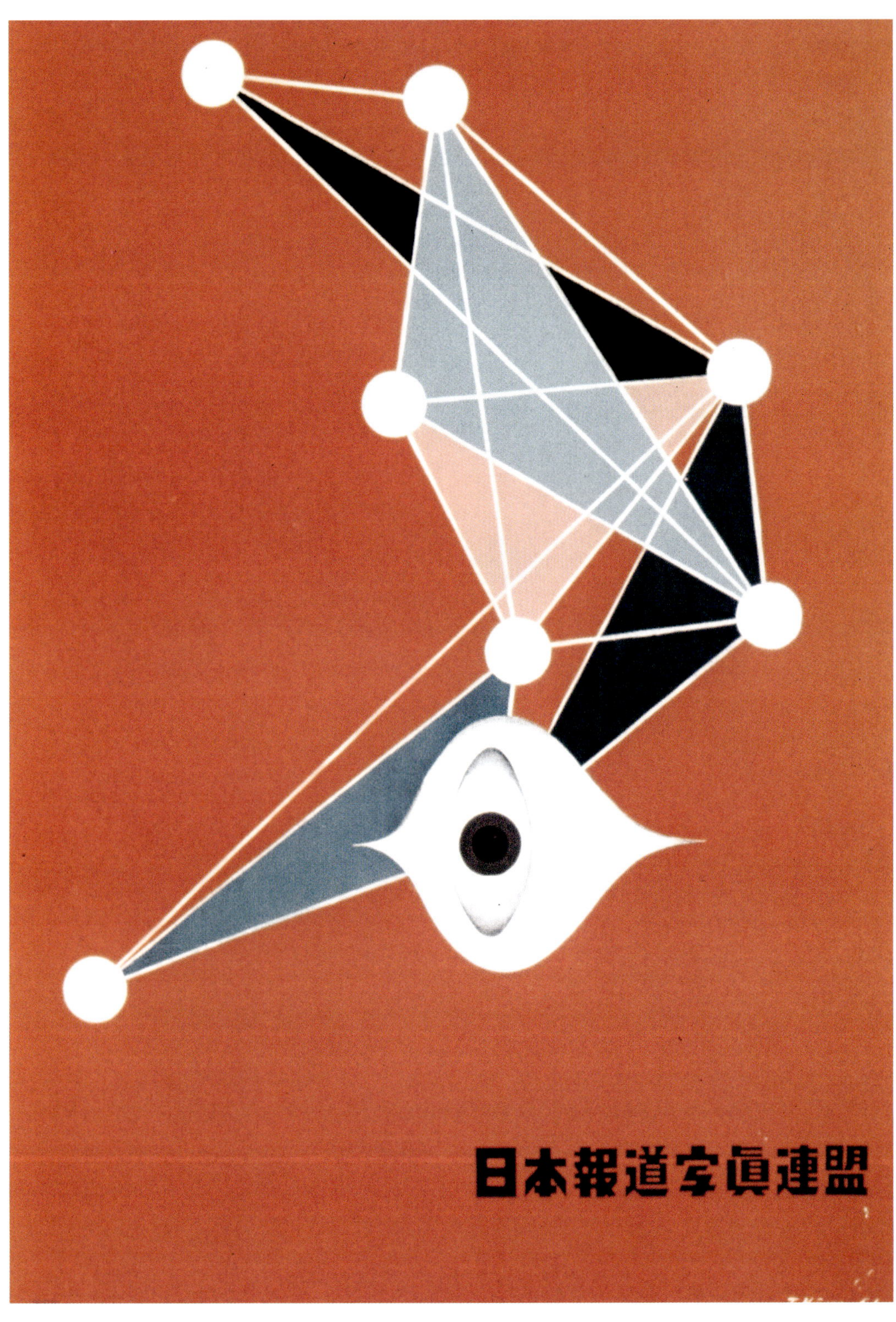

Above: **Kono Takashi, "Japanese Broadcasting Picture Association," 1950.** Offset print, 72.8 x 51.5 cm. Atelier Deska

Right: **Kono Takashi, "Election, April 23–30," 1950.** Offset print, 72.8 x 51.5 cm. Atelier Deska

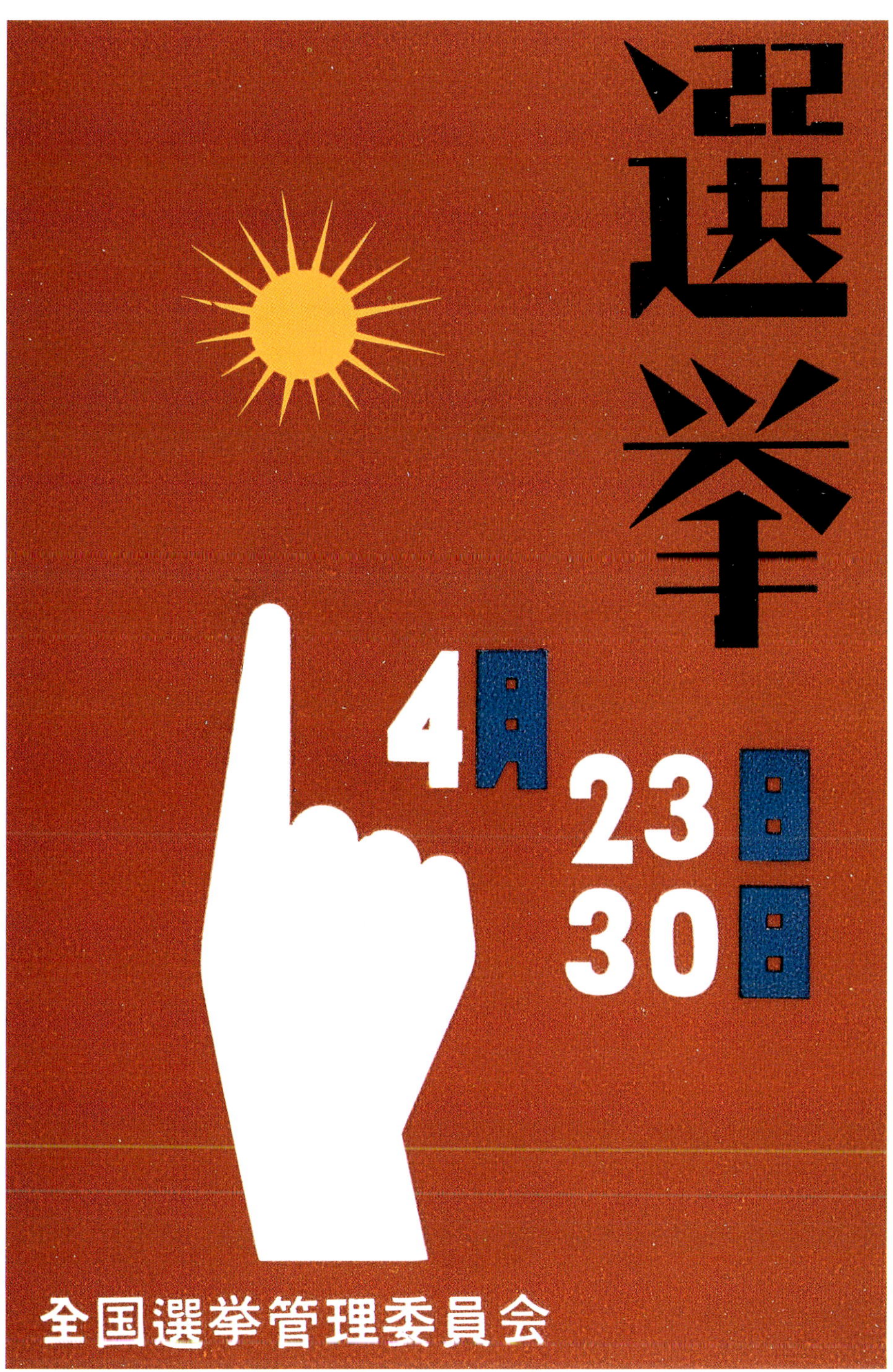

By the 1950s, Japan's economic recovery was generating many opportunities for poster designs. Kono Takashi (born 1906), a leading graphic designer from the 1930s, became a major international design figure in the post-war decades, commissioned by clients promoting a wide variety of products. The first poster here was sponsored by the Japanese Broadcasting Picture Association, the second by the National Election Committee. Both exemplify how Japanese designers were increasingly influenced by international trends in graphics.

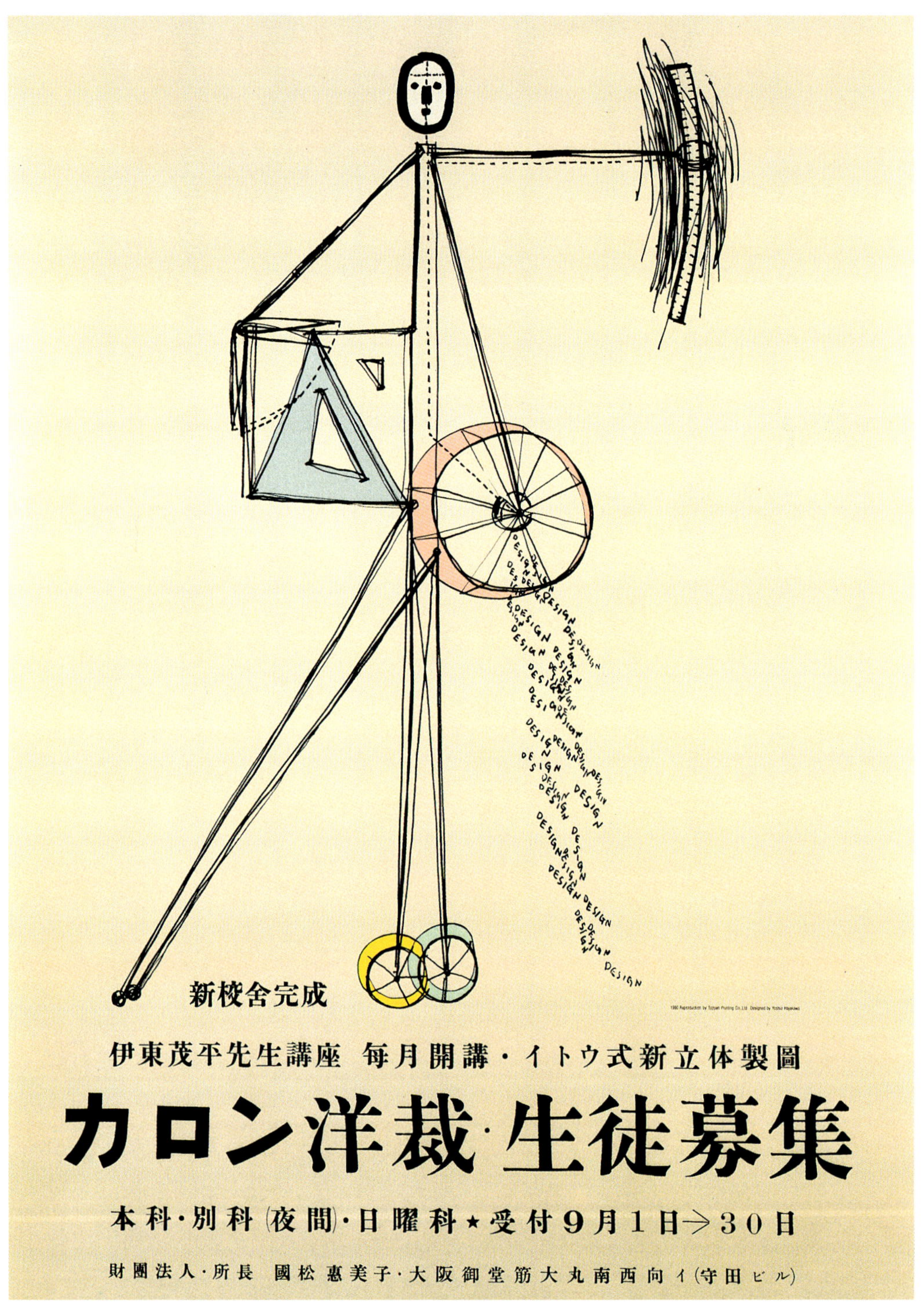

Hayakawa Yoshio, "Caron Sewing School . . . Students Wanted," 1951. Offset print, 72.8 x 51.5 cm.

This poster, advertising a sewing school, reflects the need for self-reliance during the postwar recovery period. Hayakawa Yoshio (born 1917) commissioned for this poster by a sewing school in Osaka, was a young graphic designer who came into his own following the war.

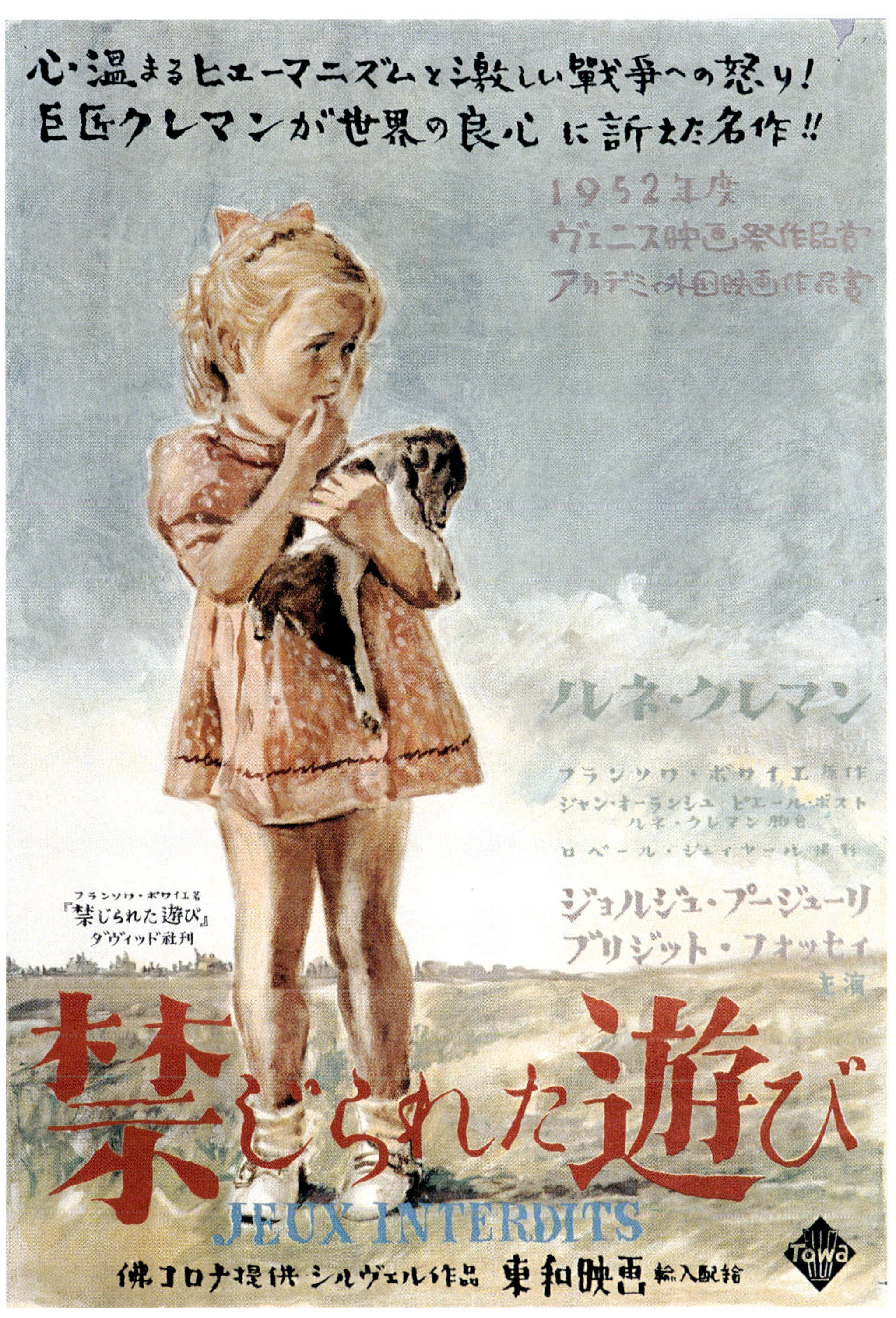

Noguchi Hisamitsu, *Forbidden Games*, 1952. Offset print, 72.1 x 51.2 cm. Mushashino Art University, Museum and Library

This 1952 film, starring Brigette Fossey and Georges Poujouly, had been released in France earlier that same year.

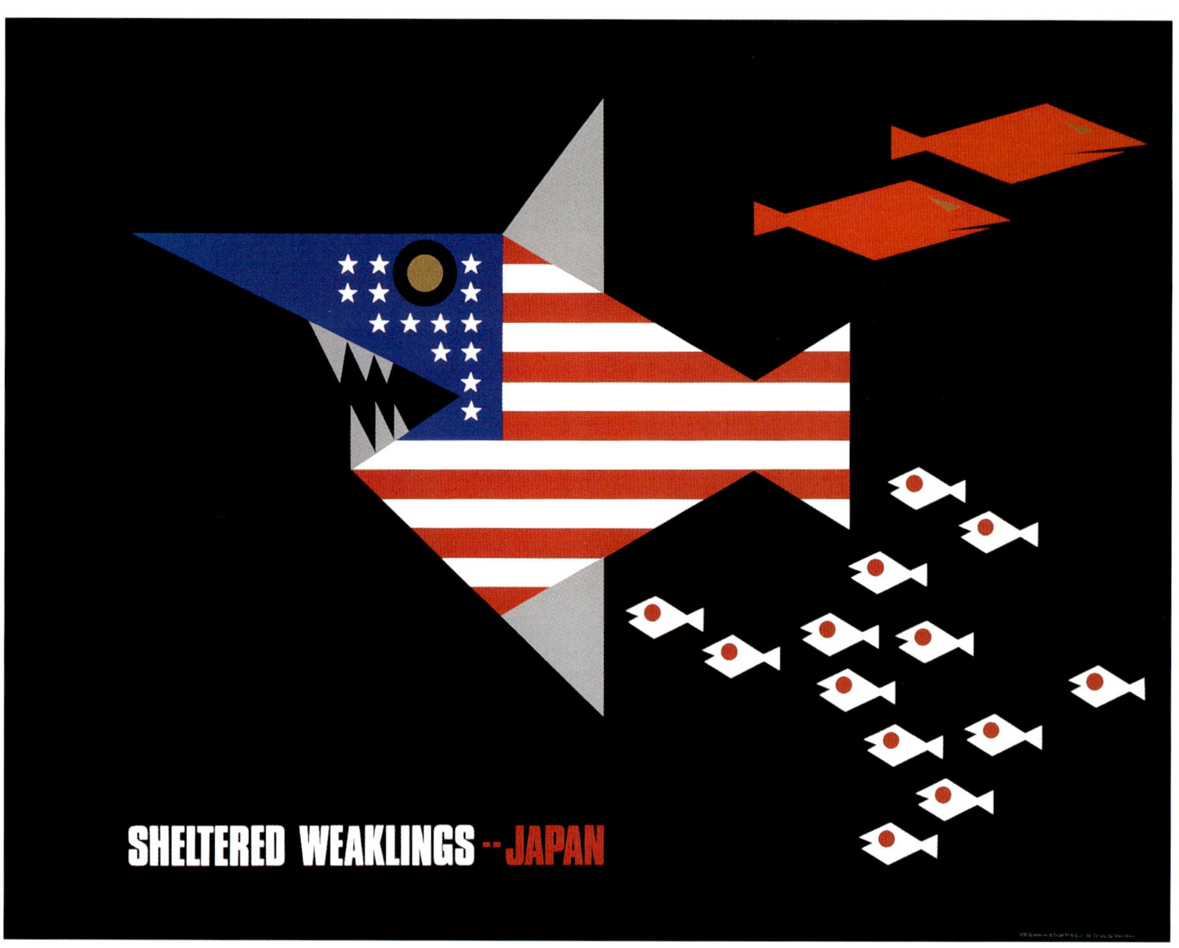

Kono Takashi, *Sheltered Weaklings,* 1953. Silkscreen, 98.5 x 72.5 cm. Atelier Deska

Created as a personal response to the 1951 San Francisco peace agreement, Kono described his design's purpose by saying he wished to caution his fellow citizens against meekly following the "big American fish" in cultural, political, and social ways.

NOTES

1. Joseph L. Anderson and Donald Richie, *The Japanese Film: Art and Industry* (Rutland, Vt., and Tokyo: Charles E. Tuttle, l959), p. 160.

2. As yet, there are no specific compendia dealing with the posters of the Occupation era. Selections of posters from this time are, however, illustrated in various surveys of the Japanese poster, such as those cited in the Annotated Bibliography and in monographs on specific artists.

3. Edward Seidensticker, *Tokyo Rising; The City since the Great Earthquake* (New York: Alfred A. Knopf, 1990), pp. 150–51.

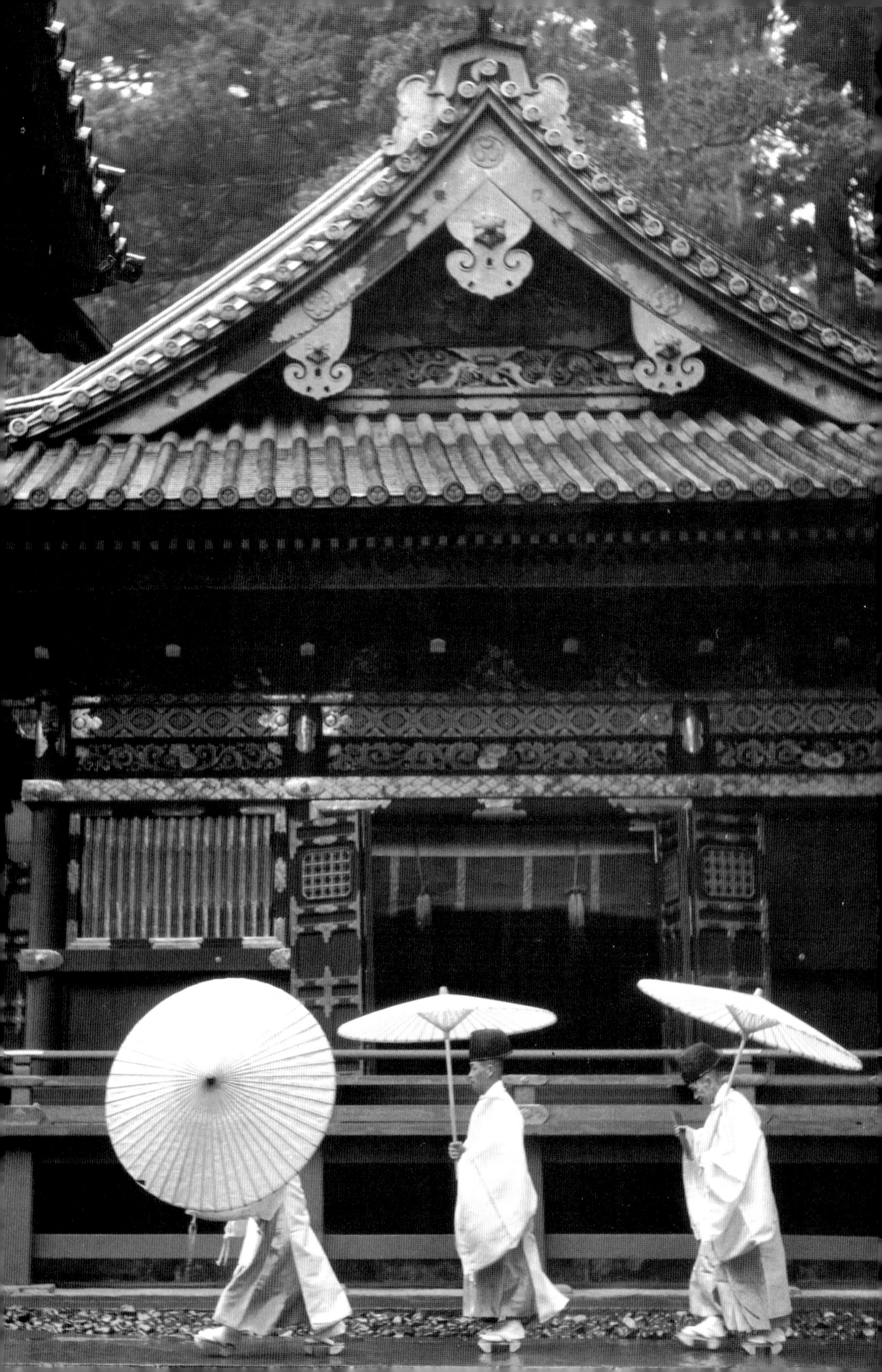

My Work in Japan: Arts and Monuments, 1946–1948

SHERMAN E. LEE

In the very early days of the Occupation, the Allies were prepared to consider the protection and preservation of Japanese cultural property. Even before the surrender on the main deck of the battleship *Missouri,* an advisory committee of American officers, including George Stout, the conservator of the Fogg Art Museum at Harvard, and Laurence Sickman, curator of oriental art at the Nelson Art Gallery in Kansas City, familiar with the new Arts and Monuments Division in the European theater, had called for a similar unit in Japan, but not necessarily staffed with active servicemen. This was to be the Arts and Monuments Division of the Civil Information and Education Section of General Headquarters (GHQ) of the Supreme Commander of the Allied Powers (SCAP) in Tokyo.

On the advice of Langdon Warner, the Harvard teacher of many of the curators of oriental art in American museums, Howard C. Hollis, curator at the Cleveland Museum of Art, was appointed in September 1946 as officer in charge of arts and monuments. As a volunteer assistant to him in Cleveland from 1940 to 1941, and curator of oriental art at the Detroit Institute of Arts, my qualifications for specific expertise in Japanese art were meager, to say the least, but Howard asked if I would come as assistant to him with the incongruous title of "adviser on collections." Despite my having just returned in April 1946 from naval service in the Pacific theater, my wife Ruth and I decided the opportunity to at last get a large dose of experience in East Asia was too propitious to ignore, and so I accepted.

We were encouraged in the decision by knowing that my past military service would give us "points" to advance us and our two children, Katherine and Margaret, on the priority list for permission to go to Tokyo and take up housing in that city. My jump in salary and assimilated rank as a civilian (major from lieutenant j.g.) would provide us with a more than adequate living, and we could look forward to the family's being together within three months — before Christmas. Our meeting was delayed by storms at sea and a miserable health situation on board ship resulting in a forlorn reunion the second week in January. Both children went directly from ship to hospital, leaving a dreary, unused Christmas tree for Ruth's welcome to Japan.

Horace Bristol, *Three Priests in Rain, Nikko,* 1947. Black and white silver gelatin print.

I had flown by way of Anchorage, and my brief bachelor stay in Japan was at the Yashima and Dai-ichi hotels, followed

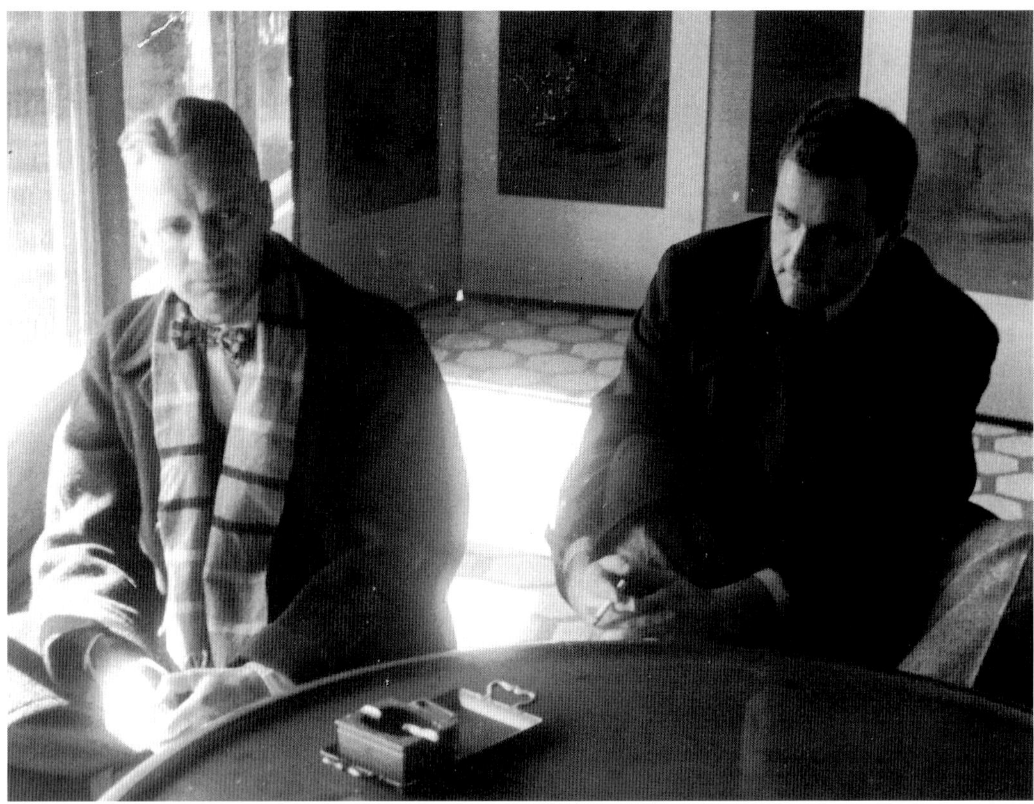

Sherman Lee and Howard Hollis, 1947.

by a new residence at Aoyama-Takagi-cho, an area not far from the Red Cross hospital that had survived the bombing of Tokyo. I had chosen the house with care. It was smaller than our usual and basically modern, Western-style with one Japanese room. I had witnessed the rash of fires in commandeered Occupation houses, due largely to the lethal combination of electric heaters, inadequate wiring, and "fuses" and was determined to think small and new as a preventive safety measure. It worked.

The Arts and Monuments Division was set up to inventory and inspect all Japanese art in the country, to determine what works had been destroyed, to assist the Japanese in the protection and preservation of their cultural property, and to encourage the display of Japanese works of art. The division's office was in "Radio Tokyo," a graceless structure of reinforced concrete near the Imperial Hotel and not far from the Dai-ichi bank building. The area where SCAP's headquarters were located, as well as the Imperial Palace, was not particularly burned out. Our office was next to the Religion and Education Divisions. In addition to the officer in charge and the adviser on collections, there was a secretary, Georgina Potts, a kind, well-mannered, and cheerful woman; two Occupation inspectors: Captain Alfred Popham, a garden designer and architect; and Charles Gallagher, familiar with a range of arts, a quick learner in Japanese and Chinese art, adept at languages, and fluent in Japanese. There were two Japanese clerks, translators, and interpreters: one, a man (Masaki), the other, a woman (Fujisaki), both very gentle, soft spoken, well educated, and knowledgeable about the visual arts. In the field we had a Japanese representative for each prefecture, or several prefectures, if the area was not rich in registered monuments, temples, or collections. These representatives were usually distinguished scholars, such as Professor Fukui Rikichiro, an expert in Muromachi period (1333–1573) ink painting, who represented us in Kyoto, or up-and-coming younger men soon to become major figures, such as Takata Osamu, who represented the division in Nara Prefecture.

These representatives sent us messages from time to time when unusual events occurred, and they planned our regular inspection visits to check or report problems involving registered works of art, basing the places visited on the registration files at the Ministry of Education (Mombusho). Since about 1906, the Japanese had had a registration system designed to protect and preserve cultural property. It was advanced, organized, and usually worked well. National Treasures were the highest listing. Such works could not be sold without permission and could not be lent abroad or at home without approval from the ministry. Works of this classification were subject to inspection for conservation and were covered by a thorough periodic system of checks. Important Art Objects was the second category — works that could be exported for loan or sale without permission from the ministry. However, checks on their whereabouts were occasionally lax, and sales within Japan were not always reported. Unlike National Treasures, Important Art Objects were subject to manipulation by being upgraded and downgraded. Extremely important works could be blocked from National Treasure status by collectors interested in less regulation, sales, or tax evasion. Contrariwise, collectors desirous of prestige or enhanced value

The Hibiya Crossing, with a traffic cop from the U.S. military police in front of MacArthur's SCAP headquarters, 1946.

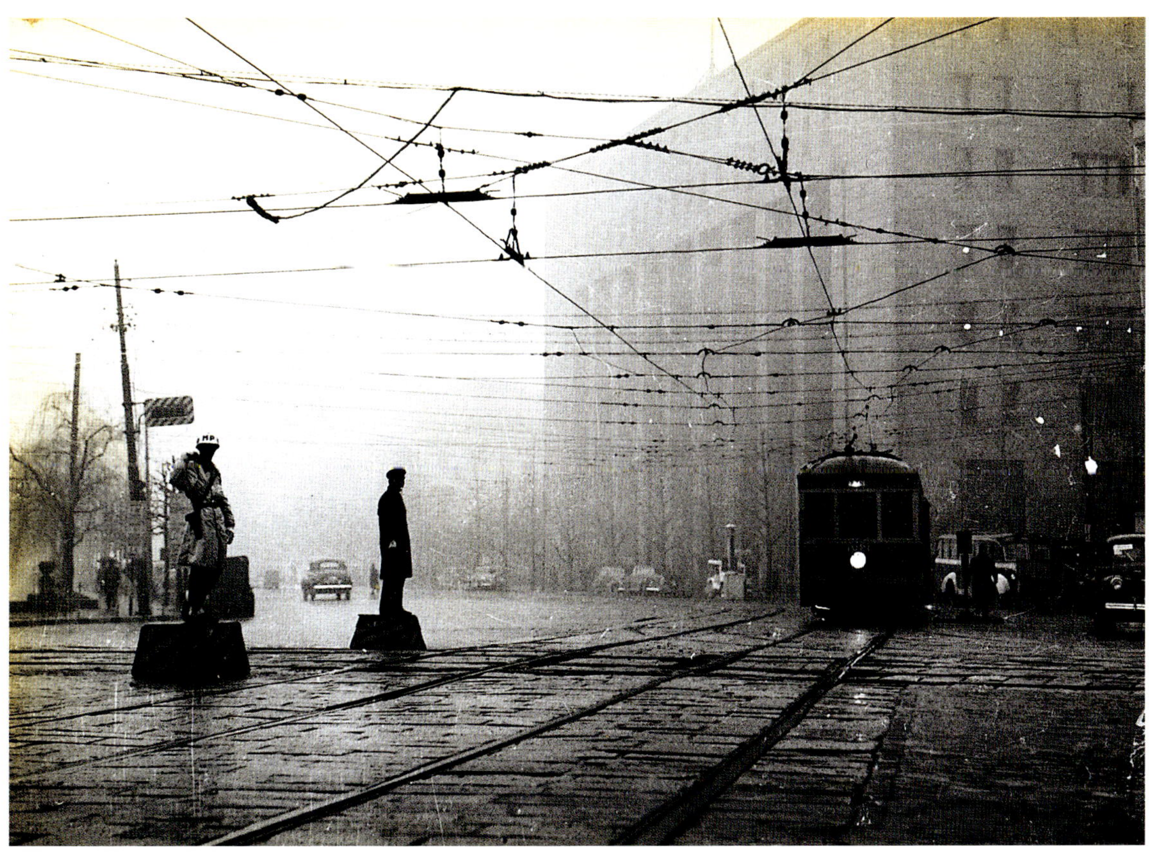

might try to influence the registration of objects belonging to themselves or their families. The division had some discussions on improving the still inadequate system, with the ultimate result that the Bunkacho (Agency for Cultural Affairs) of the Ministry of Education developed new legislation and created a new category between National Treasures and Important Art Objects — Important Cultural Property. Steps were then taken to tighten the ranks of Important Art Objects and make the classification upgrade more difficult to attain.

The inspection tours lasted up to ten days. Notices, including a list of the registered objects, were sent to the temple or collector concerned and, of course, to our representative. Visits included close visual examination for the particular object's identity and for condition and circumstances of storage. If material was missing, inspectors reported that to Mombusho, which followed up until the object was accounted for. The number of works of art seen by the inspectors was staggering, particularly in temples situated in historically rich areas, notably in the whole Kansai area — Lake Biwa, Wakayama-Prefecture (southern Honshu), the Nara and Kyoto areas, Nagoya and old collections in Yamaguchi — and the Sendai region, to name only a few. For one relatively inexperienced and ill-informed about Japanese art, the opportunity to officially see and study in favorable conditions the registered objects of the country was unparalleled, before or since. I took every opportunity to avail myself of the chance, and such knowledge as I now possess I owe to our Japanese representatives in the field.

In addition to registered works of art, including architecture, the division was responsible for national parks and for encouraging living artists and their organizations. We were also to promote "democratization" of art museums and evenhanded operation of the art display areas, especially in Tokyo, such as the Municipal Museum in Ueno Park, the venue for annual exhibitions of the contending art societies such as the tradition-oriented Nitten and various Western-style groups including the avant-garde.

The allocation of inspection visits among the four of us proved uncontentious. Howard Hollis soon developed an antipathy to Lieutenant Colonel Nugent, head of the Civil Information and Education Section, and to his assistant. Howard's working days were busy with exchanges of memorandums concerning the differing points of view. He made some inspection trips but tended to be preoccupied with "minding the store." Captain Popham particularly liked to inspect parks and gardens or the more remote temples in mountain country. Charles Gallagher was agreeable and interested in all things Japanese. I was obsessed with the great temple and private collections. Balance was easily reached as to who went where.

We had regularly scheduled meetings with officials of the Ministry of Education to consider budgets for preservation activities, particularly the restoration of registered temple buildings, neglected during the war, and the finances and activities of the three national art museums in Tokyo, Kyoto, and Nara. The Finance Ministry of Japan was often involved, and personnel were present who made little attempt to hide their displeasure and boredom with the allocation discussions involving pressing and serious conditions at registered sites. We were able to help our Japanese colleagues in artistic matters. One of the most intelligent and gifted members of what was to become the

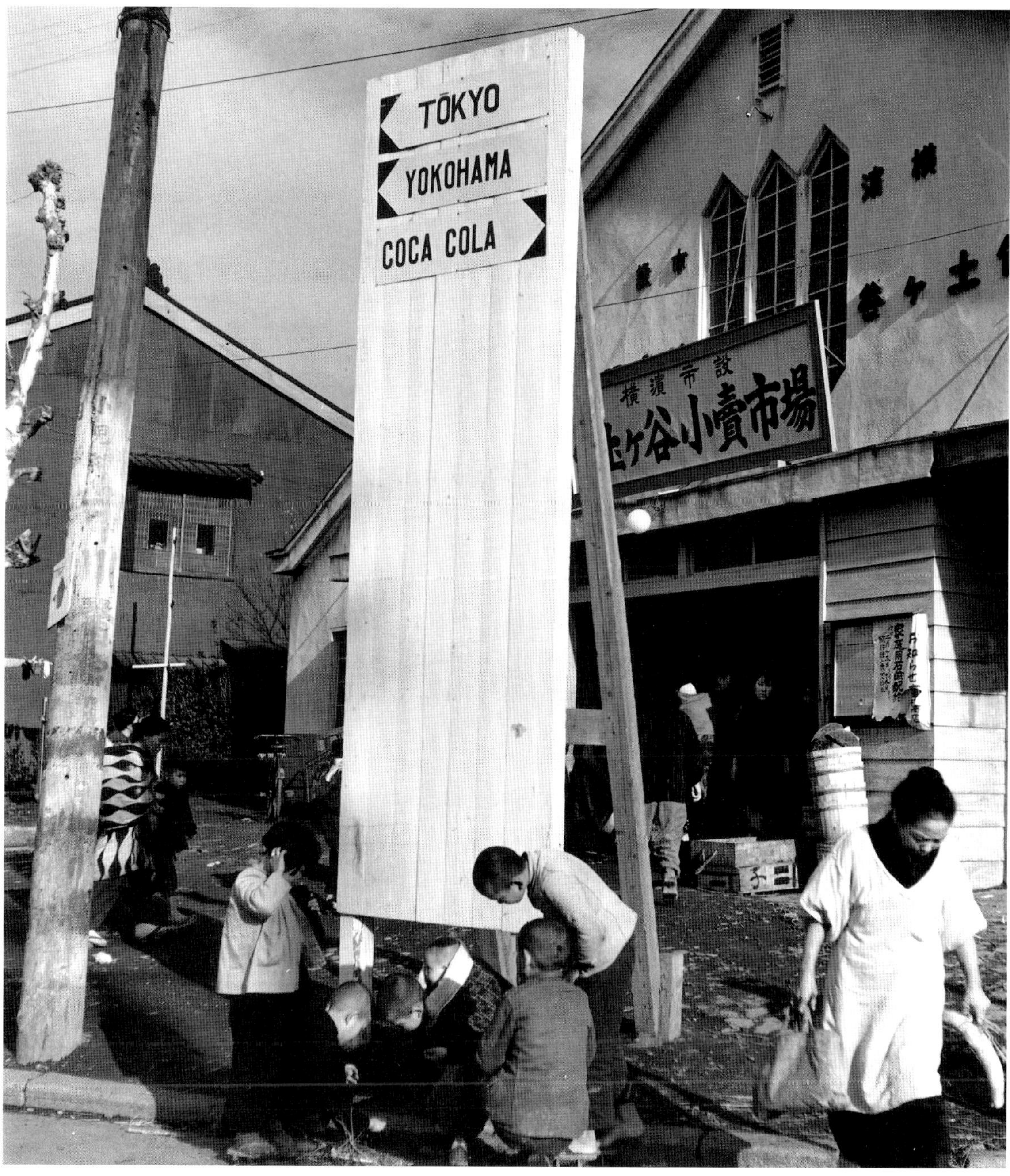

Horace Bristol, *Roadside Sign,* Tokyo, 1946. Black and white silver gelatin print.

Bunkacho was the interpreter for these meetings, Kurata Bunsaku, a sculpture expert who later became the dynamic and popular director of the Nara National Museum.

We made our first formal inspection in October at Nara, the ancient capital in the Hakuho (A.D. 645–710) and Tempyo (A.D. 710–794) periods, the site for the great early temples Todaiji, Kofukuji, Kasuga shrine, Yakushiji, Shin Yakushiji, Toshodaiji, and nearby, the miraculously preserved earliest temple complex in Japan, Horyuji. Travel from Tokyo to Kyoto and then to Nara in 1946 was totally unlike the high-speed process of today. The train was overnight, and the fuel was coal. Tired and dirty, Howard and I presented ourselves to Lieutenant Colonel Roland

S. Henderson, the military governor of Nara Prefecture in midafternoon at the old Nara Hotel, taken over by the army as a combination headquarters, recreation building, and officers club. "Swede" Henderson was a tall, gaunt chain-smoker. With rather evident distaste he asked us to come for cocktails in an hour and disappeared. He must have thought he was saddled with these "art experts" for a week's exposure to culture. We had cocktails, then dinner, followed by more drinks, the entertainment, and finally, tipsy, we went to bed. By then we were on most friendly terms with the governor, and he had agreed to go with us for our first day of inspections at Todaiji at nine in the morning.

We three were not in splendid shape for the official reception by the abbot and his staff at the appointed time, and I have often wondered if our misery was noticed by the Buddhist clergy present. Nevertheless, we weathered the day, and by nightfall it was clear that we now had a firm and sympathetic friend in charge in Nara Prefecture and that our future for collaboration in protection and preservation of the great temples of Nara was secure. I am certain that our introduction to military mores was instrumental in the financial and administrative cooperation of the prefecture. Our Japanese representative in Nara was Takata Osamu, a leading scholar of Indian and Japanese Buddhist art, and he often remarked on the outstanding cooperation provided at Nara for the numerous projects in process at its temples when compared with that in other nearby centers. Nara and Kyoto had escaped bombing, thanks to intercessions by former Secretary of State Henry L. Stimson, and ongoing restoration work had been interrupted in the late years of the war, especially at Horyuji. The resumption of the work required persistent cajoling for funds from the national and the prefectural governments.

Where necessary because of local conditions (isolation or insufficient U.S. staff), our division could notify prefectural authorities to place a temple or shrine off-limits to Allied personnel. But in general, foreign visitors were remarkably respectful of these monuments, and after a few months we had heard of very little that might require such action. The wretched state of public transportation did discourage "tourist" visits to the more remote, if famous, sites.

I remember our first inspection of the temple complexes at Koyasan (Mount Koya) in Wakayama Prefecture in the spring of 1947. With a jeep and driver, Takata Osamu and I started out with a rather sketchy map and found ourselves going up the mountain on a "corduroy" road through whose rotted logs our jeep fell, and we ended resting on a rocky ledge. We sent the driver ahead on foot to reconnoiter. We proved to be about a quarter mile from the top of Mount Koya, and before too long we saw a double line of monks and apprentices approaching from above. They simply lifted the jeep by hand and carried it to the top, where we were welcomed with ceremony. Today after a comfortable highway ride, a funicular deposits people at the top, where pony-drawn carriages await the visitor's pleasure.

Occasionally the Arts and Monuments Division received orders from GHQ to make inspections based on requests from individuals or organizations outside the Occupation. One such request came from Damon Gifford, an attaché in the U.S. military command in Korea. He alleged that the U.S. Army units stationed in Seoul were

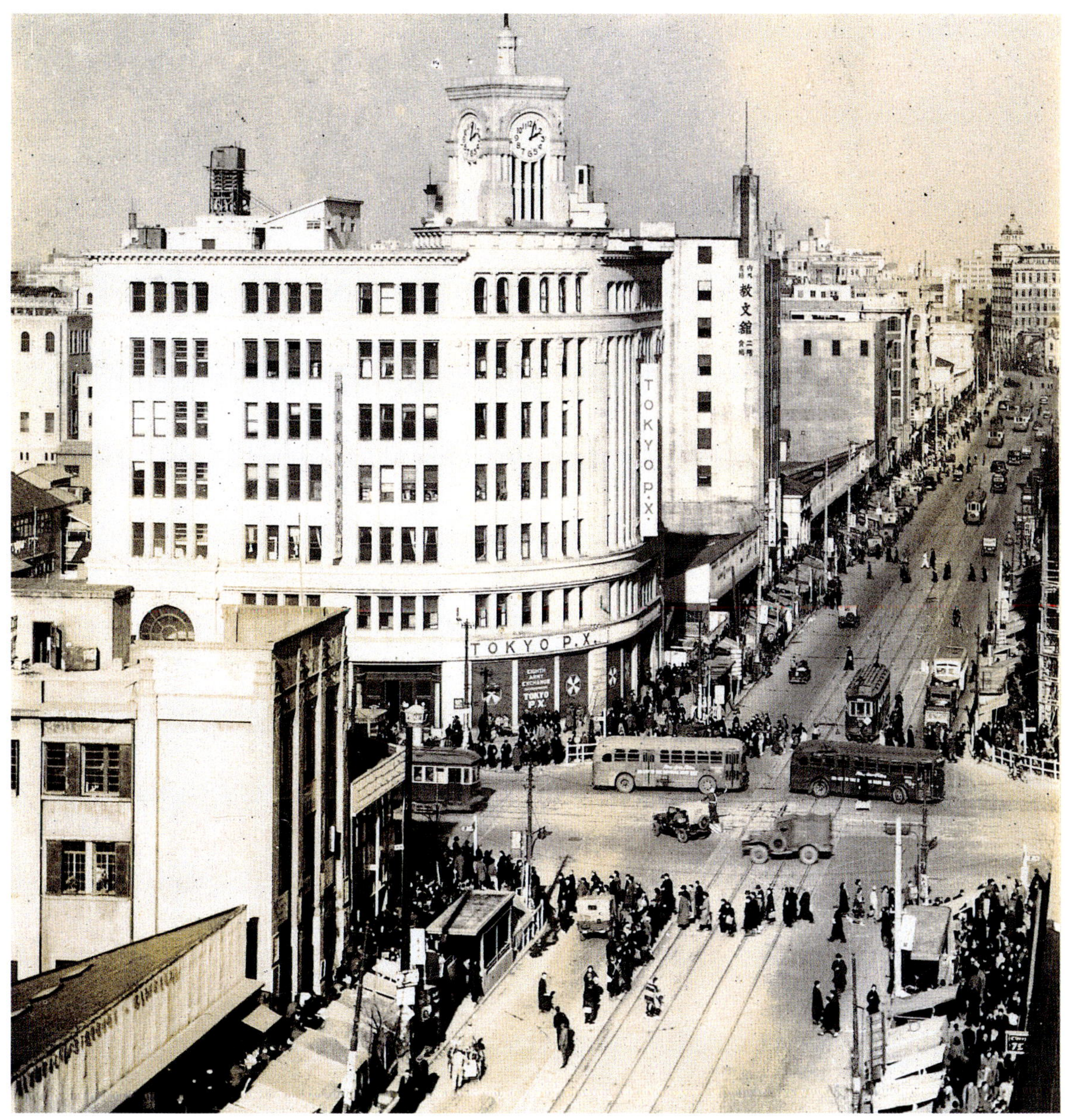

The Ginza 4-chome crossing and the clock-topped Hattori Building, requisitioned by the Occupation for use as the Tokyo PX.

damaging the registered buildings and stone pagodas in the palace compound. We were ordered to inspect the situation and report to General Lerch, the military governor of the area, and to General Luther Hodges, commander of American forces in Korea. Since my family was not expected to arrive until after New Year's in 1947, I volunteered to go and flew to Seoul in General Hodges's B-29. I met Gifford and Chewon Kim, the distinguished director of the Li Household Museum, as the Kyongbok Palace was then called. One day's inspection was enough. The soldiers driving trucks and jeeps had no idea of the cultural importance of the seventeenth- and eighteenth-century monuments scattered about the palace grounds and paid little attention to the impact of vehicles taking the usual shortcuts through the area. Many of the numerous masonry pagodas and shrines showed clear signs of recent damage. Furthermore, the collections of the museum were stored in a nineteenth-century building with no provisions for safety, let alone temperature control, causing much concern to Dr. Kim. Christmas was celebrated in Seoul in quite cold weather. A few days later I reported to the two generals and then flew back to Tokyo. I later heard from Gifford that some efforts had been made to repair the situation by designating vehicle routes away from the endangered monuments.

The most bizarre but ultimately fortunate event for the division was the result of a misguided complaint from the Chinese Nationalist Mission in Tokyo that the Japanese were secreting looted Chinese cultural property in the eighth-century log imperial warehouse (Shosoin) on the grounds of Todaiji in Nara. Anyone knowledgeable about Japanese history knew this was impossible. The widowed empress of the Emperor Shomu donated the imperial household goods to Todaiji in 753, and the storehouse, luckily surviving to this day, had been under close, continual protection.

Horace Bristol, *Monk Meditating in Buddhist Monastery,* 1947. Black and white silver gelatin print.

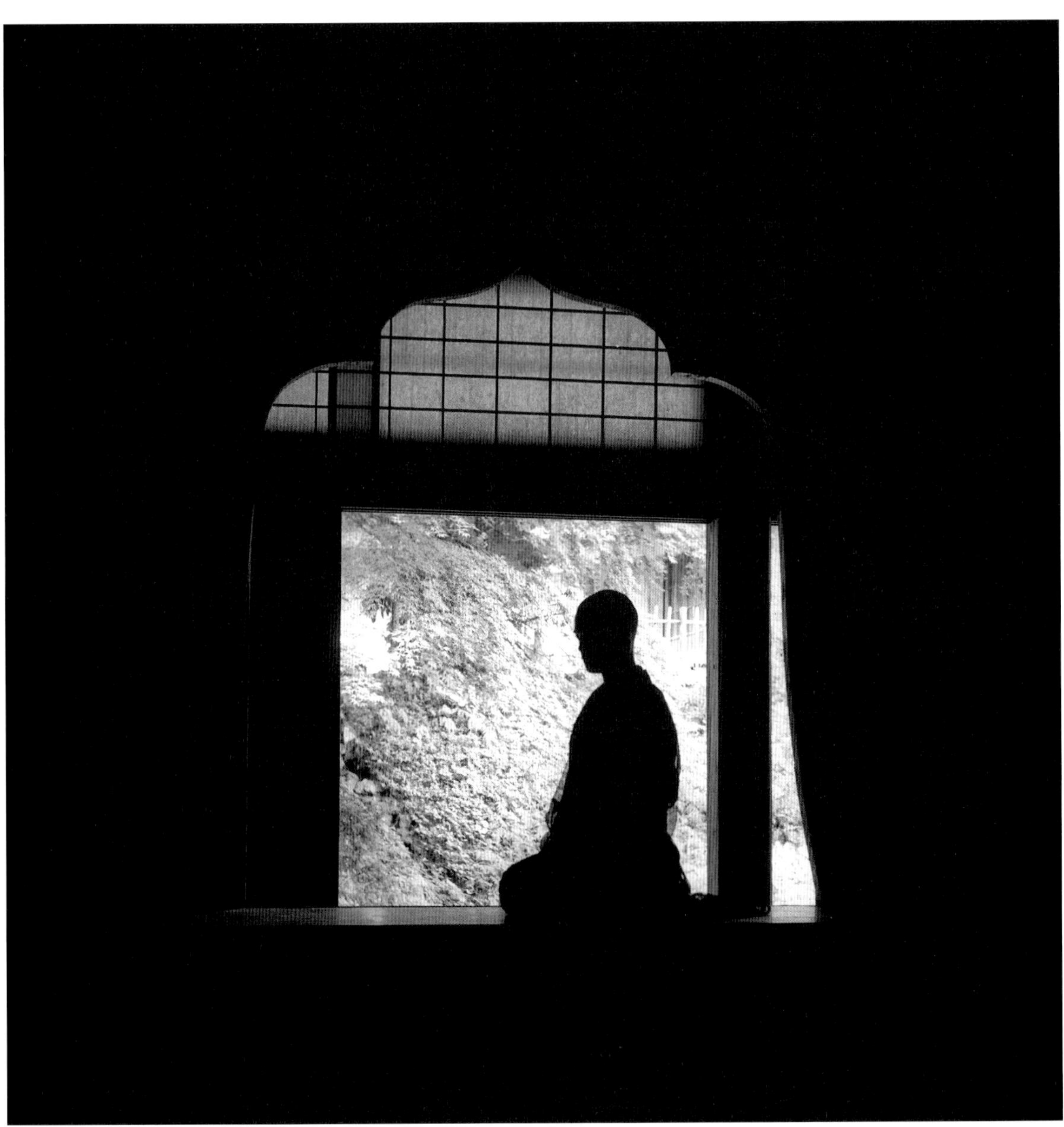

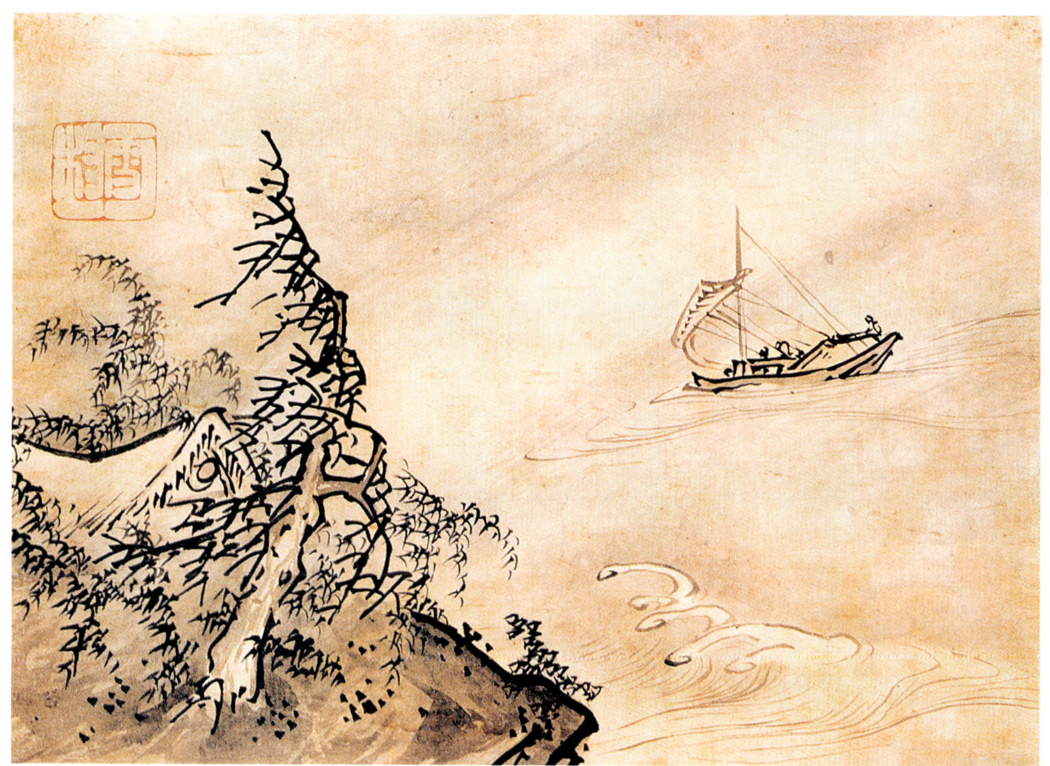

Sesson, *Tree, Boat, and Waves,* Japan, Muromachi period (1333–1573). Hanging scroll; ink on paper, 22.1 x 31.8 cm. Nomura Art Museum

In modern times, the Shosoin had officially been opened each fall for a few days of viewing by high officials, but its unrivaled trove of paintings, textiles, gold, silver, and decorated bronze vessels, wooden objects, and ornamented ivory rulers — all items found in an imperial household at a time of high achievements in the arts of China, Korea, and Japan — was known to most scholars and lay people only through reproductions in black and white. There were some color reproductions in the multivolume catalogue published by the Imperial Household Agency. The Chinese objects in the Shosoin had been there for more than a millennium and certainly were not subject to a twentieth-century request for restitution as looted property. Perhaps the difficulty of access to the Shosoin recommended itself to the Chinese commission as a suspicious circumstance.

In any case, an order came down from SCAP in the fall of 1947 requiring the Arts and Monuments Division to examine the building and its contents. Arrangements with the Ministry of Education, Todaiji, and the Imperial Household Agency were made, and the military governor of Nara Prefecture was in charge of coordination. Three full days were allowed for the task, and at the appointed time military guards were there, as was a complement of generators and lights for interior illumination. Various dignitaries from all sides were present, and I saw to it that Professor Fukui, Dr. Takata, and other scholars got their first chance ever to enter the famous and secluded building.

My nervousness was high and my sense of the fortuitous nature of the event quite strong. It was a three-day seminar I shall never forget. It also provided an opportunity to point out to my friends in the ministry that perhaps now, after the publicity accompanying the event, would be an appropriate time to display a selection of the Shosoin art objects in the Nara National Museum for the general public. They were also thinking of the possibility, and so in November 1947, the old tradition of secrecy was abandoned. Large crowds of people from all over Japan visited Nara and waited in a four-kilometer line from the old railroad station to the museum in the deer park. This annual display continues to this day and now has been staged also in the Tokyo National Museum. The report from the division went back to SCAP — no looted Chinese property found in the Shosoin. Some months later, the Chinese mounted a display of looted and recovered Chinese cultural property in their mission building

Tiny Booklet, Remarkable Event

Of the variety of activities sponsored or undertaken by the Occupation Arts and Monuments survey teams, one of the most fascinating was an exhibition held at the Hakutsuru Museum in Kobe, April 1–25, 1947. Documented by a small, and now rare, catalogue, this exhibition marks one of the first substantive exhibitions of Japanese art after the surrender.

The Hakutsuru Museum, an entity of a famous sake brewing company of the same name, is most noted for a distinguished collection of Chinese bronzes. At the end of the war, it was one of the few museums left un-scathed by the extensive bombing of the Osaka and Kobe areas.

The exhibition was organized by Fukui Rikichiro, a noted painting ex-pert, with the assistance of Kameda Tsutomu, Dotani Kenyu, Mochizuki Shinsei, Fukuda Eiichi, Akashi Somendo, and Kawakatsu Masataro. Among these, Mochizuki was the manager of the Osaka City Museum; Dotani, a curator at that museum and a specialist in Chinese painting; Kameda, a noted authority on Buddhist painting; and Kawakatsu, one of the first Japanese explicators of the recently discovered Yin Xu culture.

The greater Osaka area was home to some of the great private collections, and the thirty works of art exhibited at the Hakutsuru were drawn entirely from the holding of those collections. Hosomi, Muto, Fujita, Sumitomo, Nomura, Moriya, and Ueno are some of the names that fifty years after the occasion are familiar to collectors and art historians. They represent collections later consolidated into private museums, collections dispersed, or collections that have since formed the basis for major fine arts commercial enterprises. The process of gaining access to these collections, even with the persuasive powers of the U.S. military, was a delicate task. In a recent interview, a Hakutsuru staff member active at the time of the exhibition indicated that it was generally understood by the Japanese that the exhibition was an Allied effort to learn more about the private collections.

The text of the catalogue is a mélange of original writing and extensive quotations from well-known Japanese fine arts publications. Fukui's introduction, a concise and remarkably thorough overview of Japanese art, takes the position that the art of the Heian period (794–1185) marked the but with no specimens of even moderately interesting works.

Earlier in 1947 we had some hard proof of the success of our encouragement of the "democratization" of Japanese art museums and of the public availability of registered works of art in private collections. Professor Fukui served as guest curator of an enthusiastically attended exhibition of Chinese and Japanese works from private collections in the Kansai area. The exhibition opened in spring at the Hakutsuru Museum in Kobe City, a private museum founded by the Kano family of sake producers (see box below). The sixty-seven-page catalogue in black and white on wartime-quality pulp paper is a poor thing by the luxurious standards of today, but it was at least a

apogee of Japanese visual culture and remains the standard by which all other periods should be judged. Most works are Japanese Buddhist icons or ink monochrome paintings, either Chinese or Japanese. Notably, only three of the thirty works in the exhibition were created after 1600: a ceramic by Ninsei (ca. 1574–1660–66) and paintings by Ogata Kenzan (1663–1743) and Ike Taiga (1723–1776). Fukui uses the occasion to argue with a position imputed to the historian Sir George Sansom (1883–1965). While Sansom evaluated the fine arts of Japan from the perspective of freedom of expression and found them wanting, Fukui argues that freedom is a highly relative concept. Buddhism and Confucianism offer varieties of freedom fully satisfactory but distinct from Western notions. He further suggests that the art assembled for the Hakutsuru exhibition offers eloquent testimony for freedom, albeit a freedom different from that represented in Western art. A British scholar and diplomat, Sansom was posted in Asia for most of the period from 1904 until the outbreak of World War II, and was widely regarded as the preeminent Western scholar of Japan. Although Fukui does not note a source for Sansom's comments, *Japan: A Short Cultural History* (1931) seems likely. Thus, the political issues of the time were active even within the exhibition.

In another part of the catalogue — in his entry on the Liang Kai painting of Putai — Mochizuki remarks that the continuous curiosity and questions posed by Howard Hollis and Sherman Lee have forced Japanese scholars of art history to greater thoughtfulness and articulation and to rethink certain issues of methodology.

— The editors

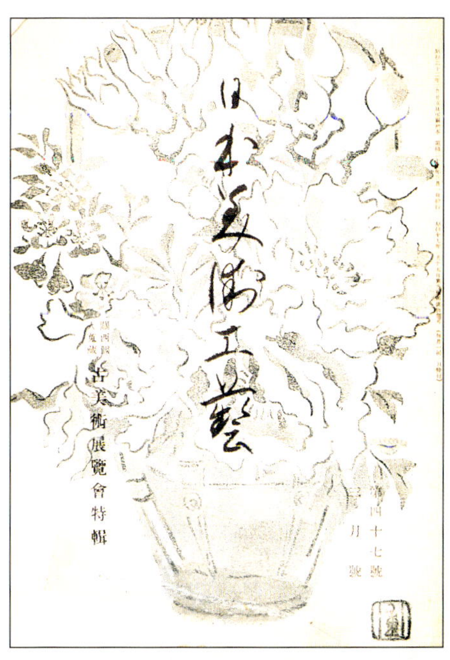

beginning for scholars, students, and lay people. Among the fine works shown were the *Hotei* by Mo Kuan (Muromachi period); the Song dynasty (960 – 1279) Chinese painting *Putai* by Liang Kai; and *Tree, Boat, and Waves* by Sesson (1504–1589) (see p. 99). There were also a few early lacquers of the Heian (794 – 1185) and Kamakura (1185–1333) periods and a selection of *raku* tea bowls.

Not all of our efforts were successful, and one major responsibility became a catastrophe. Horyuji, the seventh-century temple complex a few miles from Nara holding the earliest Buddhist buildings and objects in Japan, had embarked on an ambitious restoration program that was still incomplete after the war. Numerous inspections were carried out in 1947 and early 1948. The Kondo (Golden Hall) had been emptied of its canopy, altar, and sculptures, which had been returned to a safe storage area. The famous frescoes (ca. 710) of the *Paradises of the Four Directions* were integral parts of the walls, and the ministry commissioned some seven or eight artists to copy the murals at full scale in ink and color on select paper. They worked daily and kept equipment as well as electric heaters (including pads) for the low platforms they worked from in the Kondo. The wiring was extensive and somewhat informal, and this gave us some concern. I noted that the copyists were at varying stages in completing the copies, anywhere from one-quarter to more than nine-tenths finished. Discreet inquiries did reveal occasional dissatisfaction with the work habits of some of the copyists, but the ministry officials believed that completion was close. Later inspections revealed little increase in the speed of the process.

I therefore drew up a chart showing the stages of completion for all of the units and prepared a memorandum explaining the situation and strongly recommending that a deadline be set and adhered to. I suggested the deadline be January 1, 1949, six months from the time of my family's departure for Seattle, where I would take up my new position as assistant director of the Seattle Art Museum. The memorandum was sent up to Lieutenant Colonel Nugent, the section chief, and a copy placed in the division file. We were horrified to read in the newspaper in early February that the Kondo had been extensively damaged by fire that began in the electric heating pads, and the irreplaceable *Paradise* murals were almost completely destroyed. There were left only monochrome and patchy "ghosts" of some of them, tragic recollections of their previous appearance.

There were many more in the academic, museum, and dealer fields to whom I am most grateful. The whole experience was exhilarating and educational, unique and cumulative, in its effect on someone beginning a professional career. Without it there would have been an American specialist in the art of East Asia unschooled and inexperienced in the complex and subtle achievements of that region. ●

NOTE

There were many friends among the scholars and officials who regularly met with us outside of strictly official times. Their advice and consultation were nearly always helpful. Sadly, many are now dead, but I would like to mention them and thank them for their help. Yashiro Yukio, the dean of Japanese scholars of Western art and pupil of Bernard Berenson, visited us often while he was developing the wonderful collection of the Yamato Bunkakan near Nara. The Nippon Kinki Railroad was its sponsor, and surely it is one of the most successful of the new private and prefectural museums that have developed in great numbers throughout Japan. Yamada Chisaburoh was the director of the Occupation Art Center in Tokyo, which mounted exhibitions on current topics, and became a very good friend and ultimately director of the National Museum of Western Art in Tokyo. Koyama Fujiyo, the leading Japanese scholar for Chinese and Japanese ceramics, often gave time for exploration of the Seto kiln sites near Nagoya and taught me very much indeed about the subtleties of the connoissuership of ceramics. Both Fukui Rikichiro and Doi Tsugiyoshi were mentors with long and profound experience in Muromachi (1333–1573) ink painting and Momoyama (1573–1615) decorative painting, respectively. At the former Imperial Household Museum in Tokyo, the well-known literatus and collector Tanikawa was a most perceptive and intelligent deputy director with a gift for administration that made the monthly meetings at what is now the Tokyo National Museum both productive and stimulating in situations that could have been cause for misunderstanding.

Among collectors, Hara Tomitaro in Yokohama, and the Masudas, especially Yoshinobu in Odawara, were particularly helpful in viewing and discussing the objects both registered and unregistered, in their extensive collections. Among dealers, particular mention must be made of Setsu Inosuke of the company Gatodo, who certainly taught me much of Japanese Buddhist art; "Uncle" Hirota of Kochukyo, who was a mine of information on ceramics; and Mayuyama Junkichi of Ryusendo, a ceramic buff.

Annotated Bibliography

Andrew, James Dudley, and Paul Andrew. *Kenji Mizoguchi: A Guide to References and Resources.* Boston: G. K. Hall, 1981.

A comprehensive bibliography of references on Mizoguchi along with plot synopses and a critical introduction to his style and themes.

Burkman, Thomas W., ed. *The Occupation of Japan: Arts and Culture.* Norfolk, Va.: General Douglas MacArthur Foundation, 1988.

Although there are numbers of respectable works on the political and economic aspects of the Occupation, most do not address the position of the arts. One of a multivolume collection of papers given at a conference on the Occupation itself, it contains material to be found nowhere else. See especially "Japanese Art under the Occupation," by David Waterhouse (pp. 205–37).

Cohen, Theodore. *Remaking Japan: The American Occupation as New Deal.* Edited by Herbert Passin. New York: Free Press, 1987.

Theodore Cohen, labor relations chief under General Douglas MacArthur, chronicles the six-year period when Americans applied New Deal tenets to the governing of occupied Japan. This book is particularly revealing of the internal political tensions within the Occupation between liberal and conservative impulses, with the latter predominating as the cold war developed.

Desser, David. *Eros Plus Massacre: An Introduction to the Japanese New Wave Cinema.* Bloomington: Indiana University Press, 1988.

An examination of the Japanese New Wave cinema of the 1960s, with special attention to its focus on sexuality, politics, and crime. The study includes an extensive discussion of filmmakers active in the 1950s, at the end of the Occupation period.

Dower, John W. *Japan in War and Peace: Selected Essays.* New York: New Press, 1993.

Dower examines constants in Japanese politics, economics, and society that have spanned the wartime, postwar, and contemporary periods. The scope of this collection extends beyond the Occupation years but it includes some cogent discussion of postwar Japanese politics.

Elliot, David, and Kaido Kazu, eds. *Reconstructions: Avant-Garde Art in Japan, 1945–65.* New York: Rizzoli International Publications, Inc., 1987.

Accompanying a pioneering exhibition of postwar Japanese art, this book contains several essays and is well illustrated; a portion is devoted to art during the Allied Occupation.

Hall, John W., et al., eds. *The Cambridge History of Japan.* 6 vols. Cambridge, England, and New York: Cambridge University Press, 1988–93.

As a source of general historical information and interpretation, the Cambridge history project is unequaled. The format for the series is that of interpretive thematic essays rather than a narrative chronology. Marius B. Jansen and Peter Duus are the editors for the volumes on the nineteenth and twentieth centuries.

Hara Hiromu, ed. *Nihon no Kokoku Bijutsu: Meiji, Taisho, Showa,* (Posters in Japan, 1860–l956). Vol. 1. Tokyo: Bijutsu Shuppan-sha. 1967.

Includes a brief foreword by the Art Directors Club of Tokyo, and the captions are in English.

Harries, Meirion, and Susie Harries. *Sheathing the Sword.* New York: Macmillan, 1987.

One of several histories that touch on the Occupation and the arts.

Hirano, Kyoko. *Mr. Smith Goes to Tokyo: Japanese Cinema Under the American Occupation, 1945–1952.* Washington, D.C.: Smithsonian Institution Press, 1992.

The first in-depth study in English of the relationship between public policy and film style during this period. It draws on official documentation, interviews, and extensive film-viewing.

Hotta Shinya, ed. *Showa no bijutsu* (Art from the Showa period). Vol. 3: 1946–1955. Tokyo: Mainichi Shinbunsha, 1990–91. In *Chronicle of Art,* 6 vols.

Includes essays on *nihonga* by Kikuya Yoshio, on *yoga* painting by Harada Hikaru, on sculpture in the 1920s by Fujishima Shunkai. In Japanese.

Ishiguro, Kazuo. *An Artist of the Floating World.* New York: Vintage Books, 1989.

This novel about an aging artist coping with the wreckage of the war is an absorbing imaginative character study.

Keene, Donald. "Japanese Writers and the Greater East Asia War," in Donald Keene, *Appreciations of Japanese Culture.* New York: Kodansha International, 1981.

A classic examination of the Japanese literary scene during World War II, this essay also includes some discussion of the Occupation era.

Lebra, Takie S. *Japanese Women: Constraint and Fulfillment.* Honolulu: University of Hawaii Press, 1984.

An illuminating life-cycle approach to the status and roles of women in modern Japan. Its primary source of data is life histories drawn from extensive interviews.

McDonald, Keiko. *Mizoguchi.* Boston: Twayne, 1984.

A comprehensive study of Mizoguchi's life and art.

Munroe, Alexandra, ed. *Japanese Art after 1945: Scream Against the Sky.* New York: Harry N. Abrams, Inc., 1994.

Published on the occasion of an exhibition, the first interpretive survey of postwar Japanese avant-garde art in English discusses the context of intellectual, cultural, political, and social history of Japanese modernism. Includes Munroe's exploration of movements of the early fifties, "To Challenge the Mid-Summer Sun: The Gutai Group."

National Archives and Records Administration at College Park, Maryland, Record Group 331.

This archive consists of the boxed files of SCAP GHQ (Supreme Commander of the Allied Powers, General Headquarters) a prime resource for anyone doing research on the Occupation years. It consists of letters, memos, and other administrative files, unindexed and in the original manilla folders — a wealth of source information.

Ogura Tadao, ed. *Showa no bunka isan* (Art from the Showa period). Vol. 4: *Yoga* (Western-style painting). Tokyo: Gyosei, 1990–91.

Plates of notable works and short captions along with essays on important artists. In Japanese.

Richie, Donald. *The Films of Akira Kurosawa.* Los Angeles and Berkeley: University of California Press, 1971, 1996.

A comprehensive study of Kurosawa's individual films up to 1970 that includes sensitive analyses of those made during the Occupation.

Richie, Donald, and Joseph L. Anderson. *The Japanese Film: Art and Industry.* Tokyo: Charles E. Tuttle, Co., 1959; Princeton: Princeton University Press, 1982.

Includes useful information on the Occupation.

Rogers, Mary Ann. "Sherman E. Lee," *Orientations,* 24, no. 7 (July 1993): 45–57.

Substantial biographical essay about Sherman Lee's career as art historian, connoisseur, and museum director that also reviews his work during the Occupation for the Arts and Monuments Division of the Supreme Commander of the Allied Powers (SCAP).

Sandler, Mark H. "The Living Artist: Matsumoto Shunsuke's Reply to the State," *Art Journal,* 55, no. 3 (Fall 1996): 74–82.

A fascinating account of an important artist attempting to create authentic works of art during the difficulties of the war period.

Sato Tadao. *Currents in Japanese Cinema.* Translated by Gregory Barrett. New York: Kodansha International, 1987.

A collection of essays by noted Japanese film historian Sato Tadao, including reflections on "American-Japanese Relations in Japanese Films" and on the influence of foreign films in Japan.

Seidensticker, Edward. *Tokyo Rising: The City since the Great Earthquake.* New York: Alfred A. Knopf, 1990.

The distinguished translator of the fiction of Mishima Yukio, Tanizaki Junichiro, and Kawabata Yasunari recounts the history of Tokyo through the texture of daily experiences of its people. In "The Day of the Cod and the Sweet Potato" (pp. 147–226), Seidensticker explores, in absorbing anecdotal detail, the interplay of policy with the social realities of the Occupation era.

Showa no kaiga (Paintings from the Showa period). 3 vols. Sendai City: Miyagi Museum of Art, 1991.

Catalogue of *Paintings in the Showa*, an exhibition organized by the Miyagi Museum of Art, which includes an essay by Haryu Ichiro, one of the major critics of postwar Japanese culture, conveying the atmosphere of the period.

Sumitomo Kazuko, Binshu Genchiro, Ota Takayuki, et al., eds. *Nihon no Posuta-shi / Posters in Japan 1880s–1980s.* Nagoya: Bank of Nagoya, l989.

Contains fewer examples of Occupation-period posters than those displayed in Hiromu Hara's volume. The text is bilingual.

Takashi Kono: Designer. Tokyo: Nishikawa Shoten, l956.

Discusses the poster designer. In Japanese.

Tobacco and Salt Museum, eds. *Posuta.* (Posters). Vol. 1. Tokyo: Tobacco and Salt Museum,1987.

In Japanese.

Contributors

Born in 1908, **Horace Bristol**, distinguished photographer for *Life* magazine, *Fortune,* and numerous other publications, is one of the premier photographers of the Allied Occupation in Japan. *Stories from Life: The Photography of Horace Bristol* (Georgia Museum of Art, University of Georgia, 1995) was published to accompany a retrospective exhibition.

Linda C. Ehrlich, associate professor of Japanese and comparative literature at Case Western Reserve University in Cleveland, has published many pieces about Asian and Spanish cinema and coedited *Cinematic Landscapes* (University of Texas Press, 1994) on the relationship between the visual arts and cinemas of China and Japan.

Recent works by **James Howard Fraser** include *Japanese Posters of the Eighties: New Japonism and the New Image* (Fairleigh Dickinson University, 1994) and *Japan Modern: Graphic Design Between the Wars* (Chronicle Books, l996). He is library director, Florham-Madison campus, Fairleigh Dickinson University in Madison, New Jersey.

Sherman E. Lee is director emeritus and former chief curator of East Asian art at the Cleveland Museum of Art and currently adjunct professor of the history of art, University of North Carolina at Chapel Hill. The fifth edition of his comprehensive study, *A History of Far Eastern Art* (Harry N. Abrams), was published in 1994.

Keiko I. McDonald is professor of Japanese literature and cinema at the University of Pittsburgh. She is author of *Cinema East: A Critical Study of Major Japanese Films* (Fairleigh Dickinson University Press, 1983), *Mizoguchi* (Twayne, 1984), and *Japanese Classical Theater in Films* (Associated University Presses, 1994).

Film historian, dramatist, scriptwriter, and filmmaker, **Donald Richie** is the author of dozens of books and essays, including *The Films of Akira Kurosawa* (University of California Press, 1996) and *The Inland Sea* (Weatherhill, 1971, and Kodansha, 1993). A member of the Occupation, he has chronicled the period in a novel, *Where the Victors?* (Tuttle, 1956; 3d ed., 1986).

J. Thomas Rimer has written widely on Japanese literature, art, and theater and currently teaches at the University of Pittsburgh. His books include *Pilgrimages* (University of Hawaii Press, 1989), which explores themes in modern Japanese literature and visual arts, and *Paris in Japan: The Japanese Encounter with European Painting,* which he coauthored with Shuji Takashina and Gerald Bolas (Japan Foundation and Washington University, St. Louis, 1987).

An independent scholar of Japanese art history, **Mark Sandler** lived in Kyoto from 1981 to 1986. He received his Ph.D. from the University of Washington, and his contributions to *Asian Art/Asian Art & Culture* include "The Traveler's Way: Illustrated Guidebooks of Edo Japan" (Spring 1992) and "Water Dragons: Sacred Cataracts in Japanese Art," (Spring-Summer 1995). His most recent publication is "The Living Artist: Matsumoto Shunsuke's Reply to the State," (*Art Journal,* Fall 1996).

Emiko Yamanashi, researcher in the Department of Fine Arts, Tokyo National Research Institute of Cultural Properties, is the author of *Modern Japanese Paintings* (Ofu-sha, 1996); *Takahashi Yuichi to Meiji zenki no yoga* [Takahashi Yuichi and Western-style painting from the early Meiji period] (Shibundo, 1995), and *Kiyochika to Meiji no ukiyoe* [Kiyochika and ukiyo-e prints from the Meiji era] (Shibundo, 1997). She was a contributor to *Nihonga: Transcending the Past: Japanese-Style Painting, 1868–1968* (Japan Foundation and St. Louis Art Museum, 1995).

Index

Page numbers in italics refer to illustration captions.

Typeset in Frutiger

Printed and bound by C & C Offset Printing Co., Ltd., Hong Kong

Edited by Karen Sagstetter

Designed by Carol Beehler